WHISPERS FROM WHITMAN COUNTY

a collection of stories, essays and poems by residents of Whitman County, Washington.

Edited by Steve Kenworthy,
Director, Whitman County Rural Library

Whitman County Library
S. 102 Main
Colfax, WA 99111

ISBN: 1-57636-009-1

TABLE OF CONTENTS

CONTRIBUTORS

Cook, Vickie L.
> *child, child*
> *Damned Black Hole*
> *End of the World (Part 3)*

Curtis, SuZanne
> *Piecing Your Quilt*
> *Running Away from Chester, Montana*

Devlin, Leonard Leroy
> *Colfax and the Devlin Connection*

Erickson, Edith
> *Pets or Problems*
> *That was the Year*
> *What Prayer Can Do*

Evans, Della
> *A Cook's Dilemma*
> *Lenora Harvey Barr Torgeson*
> *Love in the Palm of Your Hand*
> *Pop*
> *A Tribute to Davy*

Hallett, Susan J.
> *Red Flag Against White Snow*

Herr, Alysia
> *Tammy and Sandy*
> *The Tiger and The Parrot*

Hoffman, Yvonne LaRae
> *Domestic Violence*
> *A New Day*
> *A Story*

Kenworthy, Karen
> *Eight Blue Snakes*

FOREWORD

I assumed the duties as Director of the Whitman County Rural Library District on January 1, 1995. On my first day I was informed that 1995 marked the 50th anniversary of the library and that there were, as yet, no plans for any type of recognition of this milestone. Even though there were many other tasks that required my attention, the development of a celebratory plan became a high priority. Work on a logo began immediately. Posters were prepared and distributed. A special collection of books, one published in each of the 50 years since the library began, were displayed and promoted. A buy-a-book program was initiated. All of these were successful reminders that Whitman County had established and maintained a viable library system for 50 years. These were not enough. I wanted something that would live beyond 1995 and remind us of our literary heritage. Hence, the germination of this book.

Early on the purposes and goals of this project were laid out. The purposes were threefold: 1) To publish a legitimate literary work in honor of Whitman County Rural Library's 50th Anniversary; 2) To offer a publication opportunity to all writers in Whitman County; and 3) to explore and expose the depth and diversity of literary cul-turalism in Whitman County. As you read these wonderful stories and poems, I think you will agree that we have met these criteria.

The goals of the project are also threefold: 1) To include all types of writing, i.e., fiction, non-fiction, children's literature, arti-cles, essays, poems, personal histories, etc.; 2) To include a diverse authorship, i.e., men, women, boys, girls, young, old, and different races, religions, and professions; and 3) To reflect the diversity of opinion, style, education, and culture of Whitman County residents. I have been thrilled by the response residents have provided.

As editor, I have done as little editing as possible, only correct-ing the occasional misspelling or eliminating obvious typing errors. I believe it is important to retain the flavor intended by the author. Their syntax, punctuation, word choice, etc., are as important to that flavor as the stories themselves.

There are diverse writings here—myriad subjects and styles; different opinions and moods. You probably won't enjoy every selection, but your neighbor will enjoy selections you don't, and vice versa. There is no common theme running through these selections. This is not a book dedicated to a particular literary style. In fact, the only thing these selections have in common is that they were all written by people who call Whitman County "home." Enjoy this book and rejoice in what it represents.

Steve Kenworthy
Director, Whitman County Rural Library

IN THE DAYS OF
THE OLD GREAT NORTHERN

by Dick Warwick

I grew up by a railroad track, and every day the big orange and black diesels pulled strings of boxcars past our house. It was not a main line, but a spur, serving the small towns and rural grain elevators of our wheat-growing region. We lived near one of those solitary grain depots, and often the locomotives stopped and idled, purring like huge felines, while a crew hitched and unhitched the boxcars that carried grain from these inland fields to the seaports.

Our house sat on a small hill beside the railroad cut, so that my sister and I could sit on the front lawn and look straight across into the cabs of the locomotives as they rolled by a hundred feet away. Sometimes the engineers tooted the whistle as we waved to them; once in a while a man in the cupola of the red caboose turned aside from his reading and nodded his head at us.

One of the first words I learned was "train." After I learned words and letters, I would sound out the mysterious names on the boxcars as they rocked past: Soo Line, Rock Island Line, B & O, Burlington Route. And the designs (they were called emblems then; the word "logo" was not yet invented) became like familiar friends—the cross in the circle of the Santa Fe, the Great Northern goat standing on its crag; the red and black yin-yang of the Northern Pacific. The black cat of the Chesapeake and Ohio. The battered brown boxcars with their colorful designs hinted at a world much vaster than that circumscribed by the hills surrounding our farm. Their rust and splinters and scars whispered to me of adventures, of time, and of unimaginable miles in strange places with exciting names. I wondered how the cars from these exotic railroads got here—by what route did they come, how many yards and switches, how many years did it take, and would they ever get back home? What had they carried, had they ever been in a train wreck, how many people had seen, touched, this boxcar? Questions as endless as the steel rails themselves, questions with no answers.

In our farming neighborhood all equipment was more or less community property. A buzz saw or water wagon or feed chopper, though owned by one farm, could have spent years on loan to a neighbor; and in turn might have been furnished to another until the original owner, needing the article, may have had to trace it through a series of borrowings to retrieve it. Trucks, tractors, and labor were traded, shared, and loaned like that. The railroads seemed to operate accordingly. A Great Northern train might have only one or two of its own boxcars in the string; the rest would be from other lines— Southern Pacific, Union Pacific, Atlantic. Apparently the greater world, out beyond our rim of hills, operated like a neighborhood. There was as much good will out there, and the important thing, irrespective of personal concerns, was getting the job done, the freight hauled. The boxcars of all the different railroad lines were companionable with each other; jostling and knocking together like a crew of workmen, but when it came time to work they all pulled together. I saw this day after day; you might say I was trained to this concept.

I gathered in my mind the names of the railroads and their symbols and colors; they became springboards to knowledge of a larger world. I knew the old wooden boxcars were clues to bigger secrets. Indeed, everything everywhere was a piece of a greater mystery, unknown but irresistibly attractive. Everything seemed to be part of a set, a category.

I became a collector. At age three or four I picked up bottle caps when my mother took me to town. They were interesting, because they were all the same in size and shape and material, but decorated with many different colors and patterns, which I later found out were brands of drinks: Coca-Cola, Squirt, Nesbitt's, Dad's, Nehi, Tru-Flavor. I brought these treasures home and put them in rows in the corner of the garden. I am sure they helped me to learn to count, as I always was interested in how many there were of this kind as opposed to that.

Later on I collected rocks, seashells, leaves, stamps, coins. Coins had some of the same appeal that boxcars did. Like boxcars, they had a date of issue on them; like boxcars, they started somewhere and just kept on going, eventually passing into my own life. And, boxcars and coins have an intrinsic physical relationship as well, for there is no more awe-inspiring way of flattening a coin than by using the railroad track for an anvil and letting a freight train be the hammer.

So great was my urge to make sacrifices to the train that I once took a silver dollar from my collection and placed it on the track. A couple of minutes earlier I had heard the train's long whistle drift down the line from the next crossing; I had time to put the coin on the rail, climb the nearby apple tree, and wait for the train to arrive. It did, and the engine and its string of boxcars, flatcars, and the caboose pancaked my dollar so that only an elongated and wavery ghost of old Miss Liberty remained in the metal. The date was completely effaced.

I felt sorry I had done it. I felt as if I had murdered something, erased an identity. It was a Morgan dollar minted in Philadelphia in 1881, when my grandparents were infants. What right had I to ruin it? To judge by its wear, it had traveled for all of those years—crossed thousands of palms and fingers, figured in innumerable transactions. It had been in the secret places, the pockets and purses; had been counted and hoarded, perhaps; or wasted. Placed reverently on collection plates and at another time slid across the bar; bestowed with grandfatherly love or flung down with a curse; had traveled a crooked path known to no one but itself all the way from Pennsylvania to Washington state, and to me, by way of a million places in between. Now, its days as a dollar over, it would never get back home to Philadelphia. A blank medallion, carrying no meaning, it would sit in a drawer, awaiting its next transformation.

There was another railroad about two miles away, beyond a couple of hills, near Grandpa's house. The Milwaukee. This was a big-time railroad, main line, Seattle to numberless points east. We could not see it from our house, but we could hear it. Its rails were much taller and heavier than those of "our" railroad, and it carried a lot more traffic in both directions. Its roar and whistle sometimes seemed to issue from the earth itself, or from the sky; or to come from the opposite direction from where it really was. Milwaukee trains clipped by at terrific speed and towed all manner of cars—gondolas, hoppers, refrigerator cars, even double-decker flatcars loaded with new automobiles. The trains were long—I have counted over a hundred forty cars pulled by as many as seven locomotives.

The Milwaukee carried all manner of cargo. When I was about four a Milwaukee train derailed just a few miles St. Paul-ward from Grandpa's place. The contents were mainly pigs—it was a pig train—and when the stock cars left the track they piled on and over each other, accordioned and split open. Hundreds of hogs escaped to wander, bewildered, among the jumbled wreckage. I went with my Dad to view the aftermath.

The animals must have come from far away—I had never seen anything like them. I was used to pink pigs—these were multicolored. Some were as red as Stubby Bongart's carotene hair, some were black with a broad white stripe around their midriffs, some were spotted black and white. I could see wicked tusks protruding from evil mouths. Some individuals were fat with wrinkled jowls; others were thin as bullets, covered with bristle stiff as butchwax. Hurt animals dragged themselves around with legs loose and dangling, squealing in agony; others feasted happily on the entrails of their dead companions. There were terrified pigs that looked like they knew they would never get home again. The ones that scared me the most were those who stared at me with evil, knowing eyes like little black marbles. Most were bigger than I, and looked wild and hungry. They frightened me, and it was not long before I sat perched on my father's shoulders, astraddle his neck, holding onto his shirt collar. From there I could see everything—the piled up cars with shattered slats and twisted beams; the groups of overalled men standing around pulling on the brims of their old felt hats; the splintered ties and bent and broken rails; and the pigs roaming singly and in packs. All in my mind like an old photograph—curiously blurred at the edges. The Milwaukee Line.

Both railroads are gone now, their long steel strands pulled up and loaded away on semis; the ties dug out, stacked, bundled, and shipped off to landscapers and fence builders; the graveled roadways growing up to weeds. I still live by the old right-of-way, but I no longer feel the vibration, hear a rumble that builds and then is out-bellowed by the three-tone fortissimo shriek as the engineers warn the highway crossing of their fast approach. The sonorous thrumming of the diesels, as comforting in the middle of the night as my father's voice, and their whistle as familiar as the bawl of a cow calling her calf, gone now. The brave, far-traveled boxcars from the

Seminole Line, the Western Pacific, and the Atlantic Coast Line no longer stop by my house. Instead, anonymous tractor-trailers haul the grain past on the crumbling two-lane blacktop. I can no longer place my ear to the rail and hear the distant telegraphic click-clicking of an approaching train; or listen to the poignant moan of a locomotive at a far crossing; or hear the thunder-roll of train-long slack taken up as the engine moves out and the heavy iron clasp on each car jerks its trailing sibling forward with a bang. I will no longer listen to the train wheels, iron against iron, shrieking and squeaking through the cut, around the bend, echoing away toward the southeast. The right-of-way, like an abandoned canal or a Roman road, is empty and without real purpose, a relic from a gone civilization; its cuts and fills archaeological wonders of work done with shovel and wagon; and of a brief time when railroads ruled the land.

And though they connected every place in the country, it was, after all, the railroads that never got anywhere. The dreams they spun; the web they wove, belong to another time and place, another world. The thread that now draws the children forth is not the fading clickety-clack of steel wheels on rails or the last red flash as the caboose rounds the far turn, but television, that full-color window on the world. The far places I could only clothe with my imagination now leap into living rooms in all their stark reality, so that today's children may know the solutions to the simple mysteries whose very unanswerability I cherish. I hope, for their sake, that they also sense the unarticulated questions, the riddles that draw the mind forth into realms of imagination inaccessible to a mundane world. I pray that the current intoxication with information will not eclipse the eternal enigmas from which our creativity and intuition ultimately issue.

Boxcars carried dreams; were themselves rumors of distant regions. Their names are poetry, and their mystique only increases over time. The M.K.T.—"Katy." The Nickle Plate. Illinois Central. The Pennsylvania R.R. The Seaboard Railroad. I can follow their shining rails straight back to my boyhood, to the green hills of decades past; and I can roam at will in that small but complete world.

In the days of the old Great Northern.

(UNTITLED POEM)

by Jennifer Lee Wigen (age 14)

Pain is what you feel when you are learning to grow up.

Dark black shadows fill your soul,

In your heart, an empty hole.

Hate me if you must,

But I must earn back your trust.

Somehow, some way, the pain will go away,

But it will come again another cloudy day.

And when the sun breaks through,

The pain will have gone away.

Pain is what you feel when you are learning to grow up.

SASSAFRAS TEA

by Jon Kirby

Had he been the talking type, the whole town would have known about the woman and her boy. News travels fast in a small town. But he never told a soul. Not even her husband found out. Every year, the woman sent Ben a Christmas card. He got a lot of Christmas cards.

It was a wet February morning. One of those miserable days when even the right place feels wrong. Ben had a neighbor just up the road who was out of town for the weekend. The man's favorite heifer was in the barn about to calve. Knowing heifers often have a hard time of it, he had asked Ben to check on her occasionally. About eight o'clock Saturday morning, Ben pulled in the neighbor's driveway, idled up to the cow shed and let the engine die. He could tell before he reached the stall that the calf was on its way by the sounds rising from the other end of the old building. He groped around in the darkness, listening to the unsteady breathing and occasional groans, as he searched for a light.

Unable to find one he trotted towards the house. Ben should have knocked. But instead, he kicked the snow from his boots and opened the door just enough to holler, "Knock, knock!" and stepped inside, the way country people do.

By the time he saw the boy, Ben was wishing he had knocked. But it was too late for that, so he shut the door uncomfortably behind himself. Near the center of the room the little boy was crying, his head buried in the carpet like an ostrich. To Ben's left sat a beautiful piano. The room was beautiful. Besides the weeping boy, the only thing noticeably out of place was the woman. She was huddled in the corner nearest the piano. Her face was hot. She wrung the hem of her cotton robe with both hands, watching the boy like an insect caught in his web.

Ben didn't know the woman well, but he had always admired her. She wasn't country stock. Like the fancy heifer in the barn, she was pedigreed. It took a lot of courage, he figured, to marry into a small community. He had heard her called the "Duchess" a few times in town. It hadn't been intended as a compliment. But Ben had always thought she fit the description rather well. And despite a few local snobs, she was finding her niche in the community.

At that moment, however, she didn't look much like a Duchess. Instead, her chest heaved and her skin quivered like a trapped animal. Ben was confused, as well as embarrassed, to have barged in on her at such an awkward moment.

He tried to drown his hands in his pockets, and looked away. Just then, the boy glanced up. Ben watched a tear leave one of the boy's eyes and race across the four finger-sized welts on the side of the child's face. His gaze returned to the woman.

Now he understood, and a gentle smile slowly replaced his confusion. From the moment he had seen the woman's eyes, Ben had recognized that look. He just hadn't been able to place it. It was hardly human. He had worked with animals all his life. Why should he think people were so different?

"It's common as apple pie," he thought to himself, "especially among those exotic breeds."

The woman seemed to sense Ben's calmness. He noticed she wasn't breathing as hard and the boy had quit crying. Ben walked over to the woman and held out his hand. Without much reservation she took it, and he helped her to her feet. She folded her arms tightly across her chest and tried to force a smile.

She was a fairly slim woman. With her arms folded as they were, Ben noticed a slight bulge around her midsection. He wondered if she was expecting again.

"Five months," she said, guessing his thought.

"Your husband never told me," said Ben, feeling the blood rush towards his ears. "Congratulations."

"You won't tell him, will you?"

"He doesn't know?"

For the first time since Ben's entry, the woman smiled briefly.

"I mean, about his face," she said, pointing at the boy, but looking down at the floor.

"Ah, your husband would understand," replied Ben.

"I wish I did."

He thought she might cry. But no tears came, nor did any further explanation. It was then that Ben remembered what he had come for.

"I'll make you a deal," said Ben.

The woman looked up.

"There's a heifer in the barn trying to calve. If you'd come and hold a light for me, I'll forget I was ever here."

"I'll get dressed," she responded.

Ben watched as she crossed the room. The boy had tears in his eyes and was sitting upright on the carpet. The woman nearly stepped on him, yet didn't seem to see the boy reach for her as she left the room. Ben shook his head. He had seen it a hundred times in the barns.

He walked over to where the boy was. He picked up the two-year-old, gave him a hug, set him on his feet, and shoved him in his mother's direction.

A few minutes later the woman emerged fully dressed. Not far behind her trotted the boy, bundled tightly in winter clothes.

"I'll get the flashlight," she said, heading off in another direction. Ben watched the boy. Unable to keep up with her, he stopped and plopped down on his bottom. Within seconds the woman came back into the room, walked past the boy, by Ben, and out the door towards the barn. Ben went over to the boy, picked him up, and followed.

Catching up with the woman, Ben slid the barn door open, and followed her inside. She handed the flashlight to him and took the child. Ben turned on the light and led them down the alley to where the heifer was. She was still breathing hard. Ben shone the light at the animal's back side.

Every few seconds the heifer would double up and groan, lifting her tail high in the crisp air. Beneath the tail head, two tiny hooves were visible.

"Ma'am," said Ben, his eyes concentrating on the spot where the light rested, "could I get you to hold the light while I crawl in there and help her out a little?"

The woman moved nearer to Ben and took the light as he handed it to her. Ben noticed a change in the look on her face. She had been totally consumed with her own emotions before. Now, he could feel her being drawn out by the sight of the struggling heifer, like a squirrel peeking out of its hole. The boy wrapped his arms around one of his mother's legs, resting his cheek on the side of her thigh.

Ben reached for the lariat he had left in the manger and made his way into the pen. The heifer lunged into a corner and then froze as another contraction began. Her eyes shone like large marbles reflecting the light cast on her by the woman. Walking within a few feet of her, Ben quietly tossed the rope over her head and jerked it tight as the cow jumped into the next corner. He let her sit for a minute, then wrapping the rope around a large post, he walked toward her again.

The heifer darted back to the corner she had just left. The rope hummed like a hive of bees suddenly come to life as Ben drew up the slack. Again he walked toward her and again she jumped, this time toward the large post. She began to fight as he drew the rope tight, her hooves pounding at the floor like a drunken drummer.

Ben could see the woman's curiosity at work as the light moved back and forth. First, it shone on the hooves just under the tail head. Then on the quivering flesh over heaving ribs, and finally bounced across the marble eyes to a long white tongue stretching for the air she denied herself by fighting the lariat.

Watching the traveling light, Ben unbuttoned his heavy flannel shirt. He shuddered as he pulled it off. Occasionally the light would zip past the end of his nose and he could see his breath join the steam rising from the animal's back.

When the heifer settled, Ben stepped up to the back of the cow and took its tail in his left hand. Almost immediately, the woman's curiosity was shining on his other hand, gently probing for the birth canal. Ben wondered what the woman was thinking as his hand disappeared inside the cow. First to his wrist, now to his elbow, then to the sleeve of his tee-shirt.

He groaned with the cow as she started another contraction. The light was now directly in his eyes, and he bit his lip as the contraction drove the pelvis into his arm.

The drum beat started again. The heifer staggered. Ben had no choice but to go down with the cow.

"What are you doing?"

"Leg. . .bent," he grunted.

The woman had more questions, but Ben chose not to hear them as he concentrated on turning the calf and straightening the leg that blocked the calf's delivery. Finally, with a huge sigh, Ben withdrew his arm. The light followed a trickle of fluid from his elbow to his wrist, then quickly returned to the protruding hooves.

"Now what?" asked the woman.

"Now I need some bailing twine."

"Those little ropes around the hay?"

"That's the stuff."

In a breath, Ben found himself in the dark, watching the light gallop away toward the other end of the barn.

"Mama!"

"It's okay, son," Ben whispered, "she'll be right back." And she was, with two pieces of twine. She handed them to Ben and rushed the light back to the two tiny hooves. Ben knotted one end of the twine around one hoof and the second around the other hoof. Bracing his large boot on the animal's buttock, he began to pull. He pulled for at least ten minutes, and was about to ask the woman to come help when the calf's head popped through.

"It's coming!" came a cry from behind the light.

Ben quickly dropped the twine and sent his fingers diving into the calf's throat, dragging out what mucus he could, then just as quickly went back to the ropes.

Within seconds the calf flopped onto the floor like a dead fish. Ben jumped to his feet and lifted the calf high in the air till its head cleared the floor. With one knee, he slapped at the calf's rib cage.

"Stop!"

He ignored her, continuing to beat a rhythm with his knee. Eight times he struck the calf before laying it on the floor and drying its wet coat with handfuls of dry straw.

"Well," he said, "we've got us a live calf. Now we'll introduce him to his mother." Very carefully, he untied the rope and removed it. The heifer struggled to her feet and ran again to the far corner.

"Now what?" asked the woman, leaning over the manger to get a better view.

"All we can do is wait and see if she wants to be a mamma or not."

"Why wouldn't she?"

"Don't know," said Ben. "Some just don't."

Ben crawled back through the manger, and they both sat down on a bale of hey. Ben put the boy on his knee. The woman just sat there. She said nothing.

Suddenly the sound of beating hooves could be heard again, bringing Ben to his feet.

"Hey!" he cried as the cow plowed into the calf and then recoiled to its corner.

"Why did she do that?" gasped the woman.

"I don't know. I doubt she knows."

"What are you going to do?"

"Wait."

"Wait! What if she kills the poor thing while we're sitting here waiting?"

"Inside the cow there's a voice that's supposed to be saying, 'You were made to be a mamma'. They all got it. Most hear it eventually. The rest go to the market."

"Well, I don't think this one has it."

"Oh, she's got it. What we need is a dog."

"Why a dog?"

"Sic a dog on that calf and you'll find out real fast what the cow's made of. If she's a mamma deep down, that dog chewing on her baby tends to bring it to the surface. Then it's up to the dog to get out alive."

"That's terrible."

He looked at the woman for a minute and smiled. "Have you ever tasted sassafras tea?"

She shook her head.

"When I was a boy, every time mom even thought you were sick, out came the sassafras. You don't know the meaning of the word terrible 'til you've tasted my mother's home remedy. She'd throw in the sassafras first and let it boil for a long time. Then she'd start adding things like ginger, and mustard, and a little shot of whiskey. When the kitchen got to smelling so bad you preferred the barn, you knew it was about time.

"She'd make you drink a whole glass of the stuff. Then she'd stick you in bed with two or three quilts over the top of you. It worked kind of like a volcano. Your stomach would start to burn, then your lungs would catch fire, and before you knew it your whole body was in flames. All of a sudden, you'd explode from every pore. About the time you thought you were going to die, the fever'd break, and sure enough you'd start getting better.

"We always accused her of not having a heart when she went for the sassafras. But that never slowed her down. She always made you drink the whole thing. I can still hear her saying, 'the medicine is only as good as the cure'."

Ben had enjoyed this little reminiscence, but still had work to do and, the fact was, he didn't have a dog. He crawled over the manger and made his way to the corner where the calf was lying.

HE was stroking the calf's head when his own instinct took over. Whether he actually saw the cow move, or heard the first pounding of her hooves, he wasn't sure. But as he spun around on his heels he spotted the little boy toddling across the stall and the cow coming from the other corner with her head down.

Lunging toward the child, Ben sucked the boy under him just as the heifer buried her hard skull in his ribs. He felt the air leave his lungs as he fought to stay on top of the boy. Luckily the barn had a wood floor and each blow was shortened by the sound of slipping hooves. The cow had shoved them close enough to the wall for Ben to brace himself with an outstretched leg. He knew they were in trouble if she got them against the boards.

Somewhere in the midst of all this, he heard the woman scream. He was both surprised and relieved to see her appear between himself and the wall. She tore the child from his grip as the cow hammered away at his ribs. As soon as the boy disappeared, so did the cow. Ben rolled over in the straw gasping for air. He could see the cow standing over her calf in the corner, dragging its rough tongue across her baby's face and staring at the opposite corner. There, sat the woman with the boy perched on her lap. The boy had a trickle of blood from one nostril, and he whimpered softly as his mother kissed away the tears. She had one arm locked around his waist. Her free hand stroked the boy's hair.

Ben watched the four of them for several minutes. The woman and cow stared at one another. Like statues, they held their positions, locked into one another's gaze. Ben rubbed his bruised ribs, regaining his breath, and smiled.

"All we needed was a dog," he whispered to himself.

WHAT PRAYER CAN DO

by Edith E. Erickson

Have you ever thought what prayer can do
When we bow our heads and think things through?
Prayer can be the master key
To bring us closer to God you see.

Prayer can erase that feeling of pain
When it seems the last of our strength is drained
Prayer will help make our burdens lighter
It will make our day appear much brighter.

But who needs to Pray? I hear people say
As they rush around from day to day.

"Pray with me," the pastor whispered
As he climbed the altar star
I shall preach a better sermon
If your thoughts are raised in prayer.

"Pray with me," the student murmurs
as the final tests grow near
I know that I'll do much better
If I know that God is here.

"Pray with me," the small child whimpers
When the day had not gone well
"Help me talk to God this evening
I have so very much to tell."

"Pray with me," the old man uttered
As his trembling hand reached out
Pleading for the strength so needed
As he suffers there with doubt.

Yes, prayer is something that is needed
No matter what our place in life.
Pastor, teacher, student, parent,
Brother, Sister, Husband, Wife.

O let us bow our heads together
To show how much we really care
And the God in his great compassion
Will reward you for your prayer.

MEASURE OF THE SERPENT

by Steve Kenworthy

I had never come face-to-face with a rattlesnake. But my dad had a collection of rattles from snakes he had killed while on the job. And now that I worked for my father, doing the same things he did, it was inevitable that someday, somewhere I would meet up with a fabled Diamondback.

My father's family business involved making structural inspections of homes. We inspected the exteriors, the interiors, the attic spaces, the plumbing, and the crawlspace beneath the house. It was in the substructure crawlspaces that my father had made his herpetological conquests and where I fully expected someday to meet my own viperous nemesis. These inspections often resulted in a contract to do work to bring the structures up to the various building, plumbing, and pest control codes. It was while performing such work on a house that I had my inaugural encounter with *crotalus atrox.*

The dry heat of late summer drives the parched rattlesnakes down from the hills. In fact some Indian tribes believe rattlesnakes are messengers from the Gods foretelling drought conditions. My particular experience occurred in August of a drought year. A heat wave that sent temperatures well above the century mark, and an extended drought combined to create optimal conditions to force increased human/serpent encounters. The local newspapers were replete with stories of such encounters. Public health and safety officials issued daily warnings about how to avoid or handle any unwanted rattlesnake rendezvous. Such was the atmosphere as my story begins.

My father had performed an inspection on a rather grandiose villa in the foothills surrounding our suburban community. The house had been designed and built by an eccentric, but extremely successful doctor. The amenities and view this property afforded were spectacular. The craftsmanship was Old World and exquisite. However, either as a token of their laziness or as a rebellious statement against the upper classes, the builders had left a significant amount of building debris in the substructure crawlspace. To meet the local codes this debris would have to be removed. My assignment was to remove the scrap wood from under this house.

"There are rattlesnakes under there," my father said as he gave me my assignment. I thought of his collection of rattles and had no reason to doubt his expertise. "Be very careful because the snakes will hide under the debris." My father was all seriousness, giving this counsel as any general might when sending a foot soldier off to battle. "Always wear gloves and make sure your pants are tied around your work boots." I left his office with a growing nervousness about the task ahead. I made preparations for departure and climbed aboard my pick-up to get this job over with. Before I could back out of the driveway my father appeared at the side of the truck and once again tried to explain the danger and probability of an encounter with rattlesnakes. This concern was uncharacteristic for my dad. His boys were not wimps and knew how to take care of themselves. His insistence of caution caused my nervousness to swell. I was moved by how much my father cared for me.

I drove the ten or so miles from our shop to the address I had been given, all the while planning my strategy as to just what exactly I would do when I encountered my rattler. I reviewed in my mind the boy scout first aid training I learned for snake bites. I made sure I new exactly how to get from the house to a hospital. I wondered if it legal to drive under the influence of snake venom. Proper preparation seemed the best procedure.

I arrived at the house and surveyed the situation. The house was the last vestige of civilization before a snake-infested wilderness. It was obvious that this house would be the first territorial casualty in a serpent invasion. On the positive side, the house was built on a hill giving an abundant crawlspace throughout most of the structure. I prepared for battle.

We always carried with us a large probe which was really a hormonally-enhanced screwdriver about two feet long and weighing about three pounds. I knew that all the debris would have to be cleared with one hand, because the other would never leave the handle of my probe. I took some hemp twine and tied my Levi's around my heavy leather work boots with steel toes. Although the scars and calluses on my hands demonstrated my disregard for work gloves, I pulled on a pair of the heaviest, thickest leather gloves I could find.

Over this ensemble I pulled on a pair of heavy canvas overalls. Despite the 110 degree heat, I still felt underdressed.

The crawlspace access was on the downhill side of the building, meaning that there at the entrance I could stand up under the house without even hunching over. This was good. Even better, the owner had used the area immediately around the crawlspace door as storage for his yard and garden implements. He had installed a cement floor and a single naked light bulb. I found the switch and was comforted a bit when the yellow rays penetrated into the inky darkness. This was a solution to my anticipated problem of what to pick up the garbage with if I had a probe in one hand and a flashlight in the other. The light was adequate for all but the darkest corners of the substructure area.

I thought it most prudent to begin clearing out the debris closest to the door. I had brought in an old, dented mortar box in which to pile the scraps and haul out to my truck. I began to gingerly pick up stray pieces of wood and place them in the box. Many times I would kick the larger pieces, poised to scramble for the exit if anything moved or rattled. Two-by-fours, two-by-sixes, plywood, shingles— it was all there and lots of it. I cleared out the scattered pieces and moved farther and farther from the safety of the crawlspace door and exit to the wide open spaces where I could run from danger. As I moved farther from the crawlspace door the ceiling (in reality, the floor) pressed down upon me and I began first to stoop and then to crawl. Crawling was uncomfortable because of the hard, rock-strewn ground. After working for twenty minutes or so and not encountering any reptiles, benign or venomous, I began to relax a bit and work a little faster.

When I had worked my way out about twenty feet from the point where I had entered the substructure, I encountered a rather large pile of debris lying on an outcropping of rocks. By this time I was in a prone position, although I had plenty of shoulder room. The light still illuminated the area, if somewhat dimly. The pile would be too much for my box to handle considering all I had placed in it already. Resenting the extra work, I hauled the box out to my truck and returned to this pile with an empty box. For some reason this pile instilled in me a renewed apprehension of reptilian surprises. I picked up each scrap of paper and wood as if even these inanimate objects could bite me.

Despite the heat outside, underneath the well-insulated house it was relatively cool. Still, I perspired. The sweat was uncomfortable. My hands felt as damp as if I had dunked them in a pail of water. The sweat rolling into my eyes stung and distracted me. A feeling of foreboding enveloped me. The premonition was that I was sitting, literally, on a nest of vipers. I reached down to pick up a scrap of plywood about a foot square. As soon as I touched it I realized my mistake. The board moved on its own and something struck at my hand from beneath the board. At the same time there was an urgent rattling sound that iced my heart. In one swift, fluid, panicked-inspired movement I leapt horizontally for the crawlspace door, clearing the distance in a single bound. It was only through extreme control that I did not soil myself. I ripped off my gloves to see if there was broken skin. I couldn't see any tell-tale puncture marks, but my shallow breathing was rapid and my heart was racing. I began to see stars in the periphery of my vision and was sure if the snake had not killed me, the shock surely would. I didn't want to die alone in the dim recesses of the substructure of a strange house. I struggled for control and managed to stagger out from under the house. The hot dry air was reviving and I regained my composure in a few minutes. It was with welcome relief that I realized I would live to see another day.

I had never looked back at the pile. I realized with some embarrassment that I had run scared. Unless I mustered my courage, returned to the pile, and faced my nightmare, there would be no trophy rattle to parade home as a sign of my bravery. I searched out the perfect stone with which to crush the Diamondback. I found one that weighed a good ten pounds and hefted it to make sure I could accurately heave it at least a few feet. I knew where the rattler was and believed I had the wits and means to kill him. With all the courage, machismo and stupidity of youth, I returned to defy the specter of danger. My probe had been dropped in my panic but was distant from the pile sufficient that I could retrieve it. I did. With stone and spear I approached the pile with trepidation and caution knowing that if I were to succeed I would have to control the situation. The light shining here seemed dimmer than before and the rocks, pier posts, mortar box and debris created a maze of shadow that seemed alive with movement to my extended imagination. I was down on one knee about eight feet from the pile when I caught a glimmer of yellow metal that I was sure was not there before. A little closer. The yellow metal seemed to be a long winding strip about an inch wide. No sign of a snake. Crawling forward I positioned myself about four feet from the pit and pile. No movement. Deathly silence. Odd. The rattlesnake should be sounding its distinctive warning. The yellow strip of metal was longer than I could have imagined. It wound around, over and under the pile of debris. It had definitely not been there on my first visit to the pile. Suddenly, the light brightened, the fog cleared, and I realized what it was—a discarded measuring tape. Further enlightenment told me what had happened. The tape had been coiled beneath the plywood, and much like the main spring of a clock, had sprung when the board was lifted. My venomous viper had existed only in my well-prepared imagination.

I dropped the stone and stabbed my probe into the ground and began to laugh. It was a laugh of relief and embarrassment. After a few minutes I resumed my work and finished the task I had been sent to accomplish.

It's funny, but it wasn't for twenty years that I realized it was a possibility, no, a probability that my dad had set up the whole situation as a practical joke at the time he made the inspection. I'm embarrassed all over again. . . and still laughing.

RUNNING AWAY FROM CHESTER, MONTANA

by SuZanne Curtis
(for Judith)

Parched, powdery dirt blowing against
a clump of squat rectangular prisons
boxed in by wheat fields stretched to the horizon.
Inside, they lap flat water hauled in aluminum barrels,
hide their pasty skin from the raging sun.
Outside, in the streets and alleys, we rule.
We chalk our plans on the sidewalks,
polish our teeth with fresh-laid tar peeled
from the soft, black rooftops of the brick school,
smoke straw weeds, raid the dump, build a fort
in a chicken coop, exchange secret vows,
join wrists as blood sisters and forge our runaway plans.
It's our world until the sun falls.

Run, run. Catch the last rays of sun
before they lure us, reel us
into their narrow world of rules and frowns.
Faster, faster.
Catch the mirage on the highway.
Wave to the men on the trains
passing through but never stopping.
Wave to someone going anywhere but here.
Take us with you before they drag us inside.
Don't let 'em mold us into them.
We wanna drink fresh water.

Smack.
The teacher's ruler bites my hand.
Wake up.
Was I dreaming when I asked:

Why do the dentist's kids have crooked teeth?
Why did the red-faced teacher slash his wrists and fill his bathtub
    with blood?
Is it true fat Anna's father made her mother a cripple?

Watch out. Larry's dad throws him against his house.
Now Larry tortures cats, skins them alive,
stakes and hangs them from their paws.
Stay away from that corner house.
Stay away from all houses.
Stay outside in the sun.
Let it bake our bodies brown
as we run through the town.

Run, run. Catch the last rays of the sun.
Catch the next train. Ride it to the horizon.
We'll find clean water.

POP

By Della Hoffman

Author's note: I am submitting the following pages for inclusion in this book for two reasons. First, because, within the story of my father are historical facts about Whitman County which makes interesting reading. Second, because, I offer this as encouragement to all to record their parents lives and experiences.

This story is about my Father, a man I love very much. Even though he has been dead for quite awhile, I miss him every day of my life; his thoughts and his teachings have governed everything I have done and do. So you see, when I get this story out, it seems that it is a very meager glimpse of such a strong individual. Yet, it is a glimpse.

I called him Pop. He was fifty years old when I was born. Then because of injuries to his back, when I was a very little girl, I never knew him as a physically active man. But, he was super active mentally. He was a great story teller and had lived a very full life from which he drew these stories.

So, in the fall of 1955, I asked him to relate to me, stories of his experiences. Also I wanted a chronological order of events. That was the fall before my oldest was born; I was much more efficient in those days and seemed to have extra time. Pop was living in LaCrosse, so he would drive down and the two of us would sit at the kitchen table; he with his feet up over the corner of the table; me with pencil in hand and paper in front of me. Together, there at that table, we struggled to get together an accounting of his life. It was important to me to preserve a sense of his style and originality. The story that follows is as he told it to me

There were many days that I wouldn't get much down because he would get off on a tangent and tell things that couldn't be put in writing. I wish I had had a tape recorder, but I'm sure it would have been impossible to transcribe from that.

It was interesting for me to observe the man as he told of his life. Perhaps you too, will make some of the same observations. When he talked of his early years, he spoke of his Mother with reverence. She was evidently very influential in his formative years. He was quite often condescending to his Father. When he spoke of the brothers and sisters, it was with love. I noticed that as he told about his brother Clay, it would almost be with a tone of hero-worship. He would admit to some shortcomings of his family, but never be harshly critical of them.

Recalling the years that he spent in the mines brought forth many tales. Actually, his mining years were only ten out of eighty and he spent days telling me of those years. To put those years in proportion to the rest of his life, I eliminated some of those stories. Those years that he spent in the mines must have been very interesting times for him.

It seemed to me that he found it difficult to talk about the years during the 1920's. I could do nothing but sympathize and even empathize and write what he offered. He must have been a very complex and pressured man during that time. He spoke of his beloved May and her death as though it was just a recent event. At this point, he would hardly talk about his three little ones. He was deeply involved in the construction business and was running sheep at the same time. Just as an example, can you imagine the enormity of caring for all those horses out on those construction jobs. Or just think of moving the outfit from site to site. Whoever said things were simple back in the good old days. And this man had to and did cope.

Surprisingly, he seemed to like to talk about the period of his life during the 1930's. I say surprisingly, because it would seem to me that because of the hard times, it would have been depressing to remember those days. But for Pop, there must have been other compensations. The three older kids, Virginia, Scott and Clay, were such a joy for him.

He was so proud of them and delighted in talking about them. The family was very close then and perhaps there's a lesson there for all of us. Pop said these were some of the happiest years.

He didn't have too many stories to tell about life during the '40's. Perhaps, maybe when he was relating this to me in 1955, it was only recent past.

One of the things I would like to share with you that was very apparent during all those days of writing his life's story, was how very aware he was of historical times and current events. Sometimes he would get to talking about national or world events that had nothing to do with his personal story but for him to separate outside factors. He was an avid admirer of Teddy Roosevelt but one of the better names he called Franklin Roosevelt, was a socialist. He could think of even worse names for Eleanor Roosevelt, while extolling the virtues of Bess Truman.

My father held the younger generations of people in great esteem. As we talked, I would ask his views on subjects, such as the youth. He would snort over the press's derogatory usage of a then popular term delinquent. He said, how short memories were; as a young man, back in Pennsylvania, he also could have been called something, for he had hopped freight cars all over; you'll find him describing some of the life during his mining years; he also spoke of young people's morals of the twenties and thirties as not being above reproach. He would say always, that each succeeding generation was better.

So to you, those of a younger generation, I am giving this story.

I do hope you will enjoy my efforts,

—Della Mae Barr Evans.

Barr

Far be it from me to be an authority on the history of The Barrs, but I will give here what I've heard. The Barrs originally came from the North of Ireland. When the Scotch invaded Northern Ireland, the people there were intermingled and called Scotch-Irish. Unlike the rest of Ireland, which was Catholic, these Scotch-Irish were Presbyterian.

There were three Barr brothers that came to the United States and as far as anyone knows, all the Barrs in the United States are descendants of those three. They settled in the Ohio River Valley and the families scattered from there.

My particular branch of the Barrs settled in Pennsylvania. Father and his brothers and sisters grew up in the upper end of the Shenadoah Valley, called the Cumberland Valley which was inhabited by the German Plain People, the Mennonites, the Dunkards, etc. It is a rich productive farming area. Father was the youngest of a family of four boys and five girls.

My mother was of English descent; her father's name being Adams, her mother's maiden name was Bull. Grandfather Adams was a tanner, making leather from the rawhides and he followed that as his business all his life. Grandmother kept about ten ewes on the grass around the tanner shed, which she sheared, and washed and carded the wool and then would spin it into yarn making her own cloth. There were five girls and one boy in Mother's family and they all grew up in Newburg, Pennsylvania which is south east of Harrisburg. One of the most popular forms of entertainment at that time were the spelling bees and Mother was one of the best spellers in the valley as a little girl. In bad weather the young men would carry her to those bees so that their side could win. Mother was one of the first women to graduate from the first College for Women in the United States. That school was located in the neighborhood of Harrisburg and Mother graduated with a teachers degree about 1860.

Father and Mother were married about the close of the Civil War in 1865. About two years later they moved down into Virginia in the lower Shenadoah Valley to occupy what had formerly been slavery plantations. They remained there in Virginia until after their ninth child was born. Shortly afterwards they moved back to the Cumberland Valley in Pennsylvania. Father, like a great many people of that time, rented these farms for half; giving half the crops to the land owner and keeping half. He owned good livestock, lived on highly improved farms with productive soil and made a good living, however, he never seemed to get ahead financially.

In my family there were the nine children.

Robert Bruce was the oldest, that being an old family name. Bruce married Eva Manchester of Colfax, Washington. They had three girls and one boy, Florence, Eva, Bessie and Walter. She died at the birth of the last child. He later married Mollie Myers of Pennsylvania and they had one boy, David.

Second in our family was Grace. She married Asa Johnson and spent all her married life in Philadelphia. They had one boy, Harry. Grace died at the early age of 40.

Roberta was third in the family and was married to Dave Klopenstein in Colfax. Bertie and Dave had no children. Bertie is living now at Albion.

Henry Clay who was named after father was fourth in the family. He married a Whitman County girl, Ethel Keck. They raised five children: Edna, Lola, Henry, Mabel and Pearl.

Anna was married to a Pennsylvania man, Harvey Snively. They had the one boy, Eugene. Anna and Eugene are at Walla Walla.

Ira Clark, who was twenty-two months older than me, was married to Grace Petrie. Ira raised eight children: Oscar, Walter, Harold, Edger, Ada, Ethel, Esther and Martha.

I was seventh in the family and they named me Harvey Scott after a Presbyterian minister in Shephardstown.

Lily was next after me. She married George Moys at Colfax and they had two children, Harvey and Helen.

Mary was the baby of the family. She married Lee Abbott of

Colfax. Chester and Hazel were their two children. Mary and Lee are now at Hamilton, Montana.

Life in the Fold

It was the custom of the times that was generally followed then for young people to remain and work at home until they reached a legal age. So I lived at home and worked for my father on the farms until I was twenty-one. It was general farm work, we raised wheat and hay and some livestock. And in those days everybody worked, including father.

My schooling was of the ordinary type that we received in those country schools. They taught mainly the three R's with a little geography and history. They didn't branch out in different fields as they do today but the subjects they did teach were extended and concentrated on at a higher degree than at the present time. One of the old stone school houses that I attended near Greencastle is now the Brown's Mill School Museum.

Up until I was four we had lived in Virginia then we moved to a farm on the old Anteam Battlefield close to the Burnside Bridge. Our house there was on the old Chesapeake and Ohio Canal that was in full operation at that time. The period of four years that we lived there are full of many memories of childish adventures along that canal. Then when I was eight we moved to Chambersburg to an outstandingly beautiful place and we lived there for six years. Then until the time I headed west in 1900 we lived at Greencastle.

Westward Ho

There were usually more reasons for people migrating west than Horace Greeley's statement for young men to go West. Opportunity naturally was the basic reason. Bruce came to Whitman County about 1888. He came here because there was a young couple living near Colfax that he had known when we lived in Virginia. And through correspondence with the Cramptons he decided to head west. About four years later Clay came to Bruce. When I became of age I then came to them here. In due time, except for Ira the rest of the family settled in this country. And now the ones that have passed away are buried in the Colfax cemetery.

I left Greencastle on March 20, 1900 after selling my horse, giving Mother my new buggy and giving Father what money I had earned working at various jobs during the winter months for several previous years.

I paid forty-four dollars for my railroad ticket to Spokane on what was then called a home-seekers train. The coaches had stoves in them on which you could make coffee and do a little cooking. Our bunks were made by putting boards cross ways of the seats. The trip west was a dreary trip. The weather all the way out was cold and windy with a lot of rain. As we passed through the towns we could see horses standing and walking knee deep in mud in the streets. In Montana the water tanks had icicles hanging full length from top to bottom.

I arrived in Spokane on the morning of March 25th. We had crossed over the mountains during the night. The sun came out and it was a warm day. I bought my lunch and sat on the grassy bank by the Spokane Falls with the dandelions blooming all around me. My first impression of the Inland Empire was that this was a pretty nice country.

That evening I bought a ticket to Riparia on the OWR&N. After buying my railroad ticket I found that I had $6.10 left with which to buy fare on the boat from Riparia to Almota. The train got into Riparia at 10:00 and it was met by the purser who took us down to the boat and gave us good beds. After the strenuous trip, that was really a good night's sleep. When I got up the next morning we were already going up Snake River. They gave me my first good breakfast that I'd had since I left Pennsylvania. Then I went out on deck and enjoyed a beautiful morning going upriver to Almota. The hills were all green, the day was warm and the country was beautiful. At that time there were small orchards along the river and the apricot trees were in bloom. I decided then and there I would try to make my home close to Snake River. Since that time I've traveled over the greater part of the United States, Canada, and Mexico and I still think that the low altitudes along the Snake and Columbia Rivers go to make the finest place in the United States to live.

At the time I came here Bruce and Clay were farming on a small operation near Almota. The first work I did in Washington was for Clay. The previous winter he had got his leg badly crushed under a bucking horse so I took his team and did his work for him that spring.

During that harvest I went to work on the old type threshing machines for Ben Manchester and John Ringer. It was the kind that threshed headed grain from stacks. The whistle blew at four in the morning when we were to get up and blew again at eight at night when we were to stop. During the day we ate two meals and two lunches, then supper after quitting time. So the days were long. We had a cook house right with the machine and each man had a bed roll and we slept in the straw stacks. In the mornings we rolled and piled our beds and the flunky would move them during the day along with the cook house. We would move four or five times a day and as each man had a job, it was the flunky's job to keep your personal things up with you. We have moved a whole outfit from one setting to another where it was on good ground and had straw going through the machine again in as little as twelve minutes, so you can see that each man had his job to do and wasn't long in doing it.

Shortly after that time the eastern side of Whitman County got badly infested with wild oats and the people there found that by binding and shocking their grain and then threshing it, they could control the wild oats. So this practice was followed in that area for about twenty years and they were able to rid the ground of the wild oats which remained so long as they followed the summer fallow system. But later when they went to annual cropping the wild oats returned.

In the west end of Whitman County a short distance west of Colfax the grain was threshed by a method we called heading and threshing. The grain was headed and hauled by header boxes and put directly into threshing machines by different methods as we worked out better ways of operating.

The combines came into general use about the beginning of the thirties and were used over the entire county. The first combines were big heavy wooden machines that sacked the grain and dumped it on the ground to be later picked up. They needed about thirty or thirty-two head of horses. The driver sat on the end of a big high ladder and had to maintain a steady gait with the horses to hold a steady speed for the threshing part of the machine as they were ground powers machines driven by a main bull wheel.

From that time on there were many changes in the combines. Soon there was a motor to power the separator. As they improved the machines they became lighter requiring fewer horses. Then the horses went out of the country and tractor took over. Also the combines changed from sacking wheat to bulk and trucks hauled it directly to storage. Now there are highly-improved, self-propelled, one man machines.

The first machine when I came to the country required about thirty men and ninety horses to thresh the same amount of grain in a day that can now be done with a self-propelled one man machine.

After that first harvest was over I went to work for old Charlie Johnson seeding. To show the progress of the country, that fall I helped set the first country telephone line in Whitman County. We set it from Colfax out through the Onecho district as far as the Hickmans and Moyes, a distance of about eighteen miles.

At that time when I came to the country there were no improved roads. Even in the towns the streets were dirt which turned to streets of mud during the winter months and were plenty dusty during the summer. The sidewalks were board and there were very few brick ,buildings.

In 1900 there was very little farming west of Diamond and Endicott. Homesteads could have been acquired anyplace west of Dusty, for all this land was considered too dry for farming. Just after this time though this entire area was homesteaded and broken up and by farming it they could conserve moisture and thus a great many acres became productive as wheat growing land. That has proved to be the general trend up to the present time, as changes in the methods of farming and conservation with improved equipment has greatly increased the productivity of the country, making this dryer area a more desirable farming section. The complete change from horses to tractors has been the biggest factor contributing to the increased production of the dryer sections of Whitman County.

The Life of the Underworld

As I said before, I arrived here the last of March and went to work right away for Clay. That spring I drove a six mule team abreast on a two bottom fourteen inch plow. The summer I spent in harvest. Then after the threshing season was over, I went to work doing various jobs for Mr. Johnson during the fall months. When winter came on there was no work to be had in this country. Three or four single men used to go together and get a house and "bach" for the winters, living mostly on sourdough bread, bacon and dried prunes. There were many prunes raised in this country and so these dried prunes were cheap. The ground outside these bachelor shacks used to be paved with prune pits.

During harvest I had worked with a man who was familiar with the mining up at Wardener, Idaho, and he had told me I could get a job there. So when the fall work petered out here about the last of November, I went up there and got a job mucking in the Bunker Hill Mine. What was intended to be a short time winter job lasted until the fourteenth of March 1910. And during that ten year period I held every job to be done in the mine from mucker to shift boss. I liked the mining work, worked steady and did all the things ordinarily done by young fellows both inside the mine and out. Some of those things I'm proud of, some I'm not so proud about.

When I started work in the mine, we had a half hour off for lunch and spent ten-and-a-half hours from portal to portal. We worked seven days a week and when we did take time off we would take three or four days as each man had his job and the company would rather fill that spot for more than just one day at a time. In 1908 we succeeded in getting what was called an eight hour day but actually it was only an hour less underground than what we had previously been working. It took us a half an hour to get to our working spot, a half hour for lunch and another half hour to get back on top the ground so really it only reduced portal to portal time by one hour.

In 1904 a few of us planned a picnic for the first of August. The whole mine laid off which the company readily agreed to because it relieved the steady work and everyone could use the break in the routine. We called it the Wardeners Miners Picnic and it has been held every year since that time for over fifty years. However, since Wardener has deteriorated as a town and Kellogg has become the main mining town, they now have the picnic there. It is now known as the Kellogg's Miners Picnic and is a three-day affair. I don't suppose anyone now participating and planning that event knows the origin or the history behind the Kellogg's Miners Picnic.

Some of the most interesting competitive sports held at these picnics and other events were the drilling and mucking contests as well as the usual sports. The drilling was especially interesting. These contests were highly competitive and drew big crowds during those periods. I took part in many contests and became very good for my size and weight. At that time hand drilling was done in everyday work and the men became experts at it and competed at it in outdoor events. The object being to see who could drill the deepest hole in the set length of time. There were two divisions, the one man contest and the two men contests. In the one man contest, one man would turn the drill with one hand while he struck it with a three and a half pound hammer in the other. These one man contests were for ten minutes. For the two men contests, a large gray granite rock was moved in and staging was set up around it for the contestants to stand on, one man on each side. These contests were for fifteen minute periods. There were fifteen drills laid to the left side of one man, we used eight pound hammers and three-quarter inch steel. As the whistle blew each would take turns in drilling for thirty seconds and as they would raise up to change striking they would always gain at least one stroke. At the end of one minute, the man with the drills would remove the used one, let it fly back over his right shoulder and turn the new one up over the hole which was carried down by his partner's next stroke, this change of drills was made without a loss of anytime. These contests were very strenuous so there were always two men near each contestant to catch him in case he passed out. At the end of the fifteen minutes the hole was measured and the depth varied of course, with the usual depth being from thirty-two to thirty-six inches. The drillers were highly skilled to the point they could strike that steel at the rate of ninety strokes a minute. They had to be able to strike it at least by eighty or they wouldn't even be in the contest. Of course, the strength behind each stroke was what governed the depth in the hole. There were trained teams that traveled from place to place as far as Australia and South Africa. One of the best men of my time was a man named Bradshaw from Butte. He had various partners and they were known to drill as deep as fifty inches. They drilled all over the world. At one time they put on an exhibition in Madison Square Garden in New York, but that exhibition was a complete failure for the Eastern audience didn't know whether he was trying to clean a barn or drill rock.

In towns like Wardner that were isolated, people had to create their own social life. Everyone did as they pleased, there was very little law and surprisingly little trouble. the population of Wardner at that time was three thousand. There were twenty-two saloons in town all running with wide open gambling. We had one nice dance hall that was the largest in Idaho and one of the best. They danced three nights a week at that hall and the dances there were run with everyone strictly sober, well behaved and good dancing was emphasized. I think the main reason we were able to run sober dances there, the drinking was done in the saloons where some of them had dancing, too. Those saloons were filled with working girls who were all prostitutes. These girls worked for forty per cent of the dance and a drink which they collected over the bar from the barkeep after each dance. These checks she collected were stuck in the top of her stocking which was easy for her to get at because she wore no skirt. Just a little ruffle was worn below the waist and less above. Nevertheless don't let it be said that these girls couldn't dance, for they were the best that were ever on a floor. They came from the bowery of San Francisco now spoke of as the Gold Coast. However, in a town of this size there was a percentage of respectable people that didn't frequent these places and they had to make their own entertainment. We had picnics, parties and would give dinners. In order to return social obligations to our married friends, we single fellows would extend our invitations for Sunday evening dinner as our boarding houses always had chicken on Sunday.

In a town like that, there were always opportunities a young lad could take advantage of. For instance in Wardner there were over a thousand single fellows making good money and wearing good clothes. So with a partner, I kept an office open evenings to take measurements and orders for tailored suits which we got in Chicago. Also, we sold knitted sweaters and underwear. This work we did in conjunction with managing the town hall. We also arranged dancing lessons, not only for the fee of the lessons but for the purpose of boosting the attendance at our dances. We gave our three dances a week, sometimes it would be a masquerade ball. At these we never allowed anyone inside without they lifted their mask and revealed their identity to us first. For our full dress dances we would have tuxedos brought from Spokane so we could rent them out. With this little sideline business my partner and I were able to equal our salaries that we drew from our mine work.

While I worked in the mine I was given many different kinds of jobs and rescue work of various kinds was among them. There have been times when the situation called for it that I've worked steady without a break except for the hot lunches brought in for as much as fifty-two hours straight. Most of this kind of work came on large stopes that were great bodies of ore held up by timbers of the excavation of the ore. The great dangers arose when slips running through these large bodies of ore would give apart higher up and throw a tremendous weight against our timbers. We would throw in so many extra timbers that you'd have to turn sideways to get through. But usually no amount of timber could hold up under all that weight. The company would only allow the ones of us who were experienced to go near these situations. We would usually work in relays from five o'clock in the morning to the following two a.m., but no miner would go near these stopes between two and five as that is the time they would always cave in. I don't know the exact reason of this but I do know these stopes would start talking to you about one in the morning and you'd better get out of there, then they'd quiet down about five. After that time they would be reasonably safe until the following morning. Scientists say it has something to do with the tides. Another thing we were very careful about when working around these caving stopes was not to loiter in a main tunnel leading to the outside. If we stopped to eat or rest we would do it in a blind drift. We knew that if a stope did cave the rush of air would kill you against the walls of those main tunnels for air being a solid body moves any object toward the outside and it would pick a man up like a butterfly.

The only lights we had to work by were candles which we either wore on our hats or stuck in the walls close to our work. We would pick up about four apiece when we went in in the mornings to last us for the day. In reality there were very few accidents in the mine. It was well run and precautions of all kinds were taken to prevent accidents but naturally in such hazardous work there were bound to be some. As it turned out one of the most harrowing experiences in my life happened there in the mine one day. A "Cousin Jack" and I were working side by side when a piece of falling lead struck him on the head. He was badly injured and unconscious and it was quite a job to get an unconscious man out. Another fellow and I had to take him down several hundred feet in a very narrow three by four foot cribbed manway. Then after we got down the manway we had to take him down another six hundred feet on a timber skip which was set at a sixty-five degree angle. It was only big enough for the three of us to get on. It was very dark going down on this and we held the old fellow in our arms between us. About half way down the old man died there in our arms and the other man went into complete hysteria. He tried to get off which would have meant sure death for him and no doubt threw the skip off the track so that it would have killed me, too. So there I was on that slow moving skip set at a sixty-five degree angle with one dead man in my arms and one completely hysterical man gripped with my two hands. Believe you me, I was plenty glad to get to the bottom where there was ambulatory service waiting.

From Minerals to Mules

Although I like the mining work I could see no future in it being the kind of life that it was. The town itself was not the most desirable to live in and the air and dust in the mine was very unhealthy. So in 1908 I put my savings in with Bruce and we rented a block of land south of Hooper from the McGregor Land and Livestock Co. Some of that land had raised one crop and some we broke out. We used all mules and for years I operated with eleven eight-mule teams. And many of those mules I formed a lot of affection for. Bruce and his family moved there and I worked there during the work seasons for the following two years and went back to the mines during the winter months. In March of 1910, I drew my time from the mine for the last time and have raised wheat continuously ever since.

I lived there on the ranch with Bruce and Molly until September of 1911, when we rented the old Marley place at Mockenema. They moved up there and left me to "bach" which I did, but all the time trying to convince Miss Della May Harvey that she wanted to marry me. On December 28, 1911, May and I were married and set up housekeeping on the McGregor ranch. That ended my "baching", thank the Lord.

Bruce and I continued to operate the two places together for the next two years. We were able to use the same men and mules on my place, then send them to him because of the later season at Mockenema. This proved to be a profitable arrangement over this period of years and we made a nice piece of money. On January the first 1914 we decided we were financially strong enough so that we could operate separately. Bruce the Mockenema place and I kept the McGregor ranch.

May's and my first baby was born in November of 1912. But due to the lack of the present day medical knowledge we lost him in birth. Our second, Virginia, was born in April of 1914. We then lost another little girl in birth. On August 21, 1916 our son, Scott, was born. Scottie was one of the first Cesarean babies to be born. In June of 1919 Clay came along, also a Cesarean child.

In 1914, I purchased my first piece of United States real estate. I say United States because for several years previous I had owned a half section of raw land in Alberta, Canada. But in 1914 together with Clay we bought two thousand acres of pasture land from McGregors. That piece of land is what we still call Woodgulch. Clay and I stocked it with around two hundred head of cattle for two years until he needed his money to buy a piece of land that adjoined his place near Pullman. I gave him a check for his half which amounted to ten thousand dollars. I thought that check was the largest ever written, since then I have found out differently. In recalling the time Clay and I run cattle together brings back a lot of memories. He used to buy small bunches of cattle in the upper end of Whitman County and drive them down. One time he and his old dog were bringing a bunch down and as it always took at least two days, he stopped for the night at a farm along the way. He went to the house to ask for hay for his cattle and a bed and a meal for himself. The young woman there said, why no, he couldn't stay there, her husband was gone and she was alone. So Clay set her right by bluntly saying that all he needed was some hay for his old cows.

Another time during that two year period he and I were making a late fall round-up of calves for branding. We had ridden all day in cold wet, miserable weather and finally got them in the corral around three o'clock. I began to loosen my rope and tighten my cinch to go to work on the calves. Clay being older wasn't being so enthusiastic about it. Finally he says, "Wait a minute, maybe you can take this but I'm too old. I'm going to have to have something under my belt 'fore I can help with this job." So I dropped my work and started to ride the mile to the house. As I rode off he said, "Don't bother with much, just a sandwich." So when I came back I had a basket in which May being who she was, had packed not only that sandwich but also a half gallon of hot oyster stew, a half gallon of hot coffee, the biggest part of a fried chicken, plenty of bread and butter and a whole hot mince pie. When Clay looked in that basket he gasped and said, "My God man, the two of us can't eat a fourth of all that." But we started off with a good big drink of whiskey and it wasn't long before the whole lunch had disappeared. When he'd finished, Clay got up, stretched himself, rubbed his stomach and being one of the best practical ropers in the country, he looped his rope around over his head and said "Boy, can I go get 'em now!"

Up to this point of my life this story has been fairly easy to relate. But about 1916 I went into a partnership with Charlie McKenzie and things got involved then. Charlie and I formed this partnership for the purpose of running sheep and also for constructing roads. The two of us stayed partners until 1922 then I continued the operations as an individual.

In the sheep business we had two bands of ewes. I had the range land on both sides of the Palouse River from the falls to the mouth then also the pasture on the north side of the Snake from the mouth of the Palouse up to Riparia. We used this range for winter feeding then drive to the mountains for summer pasture. While in the sheep business, one day I drove into a camp in the mountains and I found my old sheep herder scratched from head to food. After questioning him this is the story I got. He had gone out from his camp with a lit-

tle bucket to pick some berries which were growing thick in a steep
little ravine close by. As he picked he found a log which had fallen
across the gulch and there were berry bushes growing up around this
log so he started picking his way across the log. As he got close to
the center he sensed that someone was near. Just as he raised his
head to look, a big brown bear was also picking berries on the same
log and he looked up at the same time. They were only about two
feet apart and it scared them both. So with an "oof" from both of
them, they threw their berries in the air and fell off the log down
through all that heavy brush both ending up in the bottom of the
ravine still only two feet apart. They each took to the opposite side
and when I saw the sheepherder he had the scratches to verify his
story.

During the time I was in construction work I contracted and built
many of the roads that you travel on here in these four Northwest
states. The construction work was very interesting. We met a lot of
people and made lifelong friends. The life itself is similar to the kind
of life a gypsy lives. Most of the time we lived in tents in a camp.
Sometimes when we'd get into a late fall job it would get as cold as
ten below zero but it seemed like no one ever caught a cold. Our
three kids, Virginia, Scottie and Clay were with us a great deal of the
time and some years they went to as many four different schools.
Besides our own there were other families following the construction work. There were around twenty-five youngsters in camp which
made it hard on some of the rural schools that they went to.

Construction work of any kind is always hazardous and we had
our share of accidents. However, I always had industrial insurance
with the Aetna Company and one time a fellow was killed by an
early morning train and his wife had her check that same night.
Another man was killed by a fast passenger train down at Lewiston.
Then there was the kid who lived near the job out of Pullman who
stole some of our dynamite caps and hit them with a hammer, blowing his hand off. One of the closest calls we had was the time one of
our trucks loaded with five tons of dynamite lost his brakes on top of
the hill going into Pullman. He went down the main street of
Pullman about seventy miles an hour but luckily it was three o'clock
in the morning and the streets were clear.

All of our working power at that time was horses and mules

especially for the grading. We worked as many as three hundred head at one time. Also among our equipment were five of the first big GMC trucks. Those trucks were the very latest thing. They had hard rubber tires and they were really sailing when they went down the road eighteen miles an hour. When we bought two of them they set us back the sum of six thousand dollars apiece. We used the trucks for hauling rock and dirt and when we'd get on a job where we needed more trucks we would hire them.

You run into all kinds of people and all kinds of situations in a business like this. One time we moved to a new site and I just had to have a quarry but it stood right behind a man's barn. It was just an average barn for thirty head of horses but the owner was very skeptical about the blasting injuring his barn. He finally consented to sell the quarry to me after I had assured him that the blasting would not hurt the barn. When my powder man, Swede Jack, came to load the quarry he says, boss how about the barn. I told him, Jack, raise her up and turn her over. Swede Jack shrugged his shoulders and went to work. This quarry was in Washington but the day the shot was pulled I was in California. By the time the smoke was settled both from the shot and the farmer, the disturbance quieted down, mostly because there was a carpenter, with five men and a truck load of lumber standing there. Seeing the argument the carpenter told the farmer that Mr. Barr had made arrangements six weeks before with him to put this barn back in good shape even if it had to be built from the ground up. There's a time in construction work you have to have certain properties and sometimes a few lies are preferable in place of a delayed condemnation court suit.

While I was still in partners with McKenzie we rocked part of the Lewiston Grade. Then we had work up at Sandpoint, Idaho. We spent most of our time in Whitman County though with jobs at Central Ferry, Endicott and a lot of work around Tekoa, Farmington and Oakesdale.

The first job that I contracted as an individual was over at Kendrick, Idaho. That was a good job. Then we moved early in 1923 to Genessee and surfaced from Moscow to the top of the Lewiston Grade. We had a miserable time on that job. It was an especially rainy season and we ran into a quarry of bad rock. The kind of rock that we had to use always controlled the economy of a job. The finer the rock, the better. One time I turned a job down that I should have taken because it had especially good rock on it. Charlie Joslin offered this job one day in Spokane where a group of us contractors were having lunch in our headquarter rooms in the Spokane Hotel. We kept headquarters there so we could meet to trade and lease equipment from one another also we would sub or lease certain parts of the jobs. This job that Charlie offered me was down at Shaniko, Oregon, to surface some twenty-five miles of the Dalles California Highway. I told Charlie no, that I had more than I could do just then. Afterwards when I drove over that stretch of road and saw the two quarries that the rock had come out of, I knew I had dropped twenty-five thousand dollars by shaking my head when I should have been nodding it.

After finishing the Genessee job we moved the whole outfit to Deep Creek along about the first of August. We built eight miles of the Coulee Height road there. There were a number of cuts in that job and a lot of heavy work so that we got late in the fall and had to hold the job over winter.

So financially 1923 was a bad year. We lost money on both construction jobs but I guess as the old saying goes, trouble never comes singly. For about the first of June, May took sick with acute Bright's Disease and was sick for nine long weeks until she died the first of August. So I ended that year with three children without a mother and a bunch of debts.

But in February of '24, we took on the Deer Park-Milan contract which proved to be a very pleasant job because we made money. Then after the Deer Park job we surfaced from Palouse to Pullman. The competition for that job was so keen that we got the contract for a quarter a cent a yard less than the next bidder. There were some ten bidders on that job and there wasn't a nickel's spread between any of the bids. Also here without moving camp or quarry we picked up the work of rocking down the Four-Mile road, which was pay dirt as there was very little expense. Then we moved into Colfax where we spent the winter working and until the fifth of July in 1925. In Colfax we did a lot of work surfacing many of the streets. Also we furnished rock for individuals and for Whitman County. It was here that we graded and rocked some eight miles of the Almota road in thirty days which was unbelievably fast for that time.

After we left Colfax in '25 we moved down to Condon, Oregon. We had a Federal Aid job there surfacing forty miles of the John Day highway for the State of Oregon and also did work for Gilliam County. When we left Condon on Thanksgiving we had all our bills paid and everybody had paid us.

After we finished at Condon we spent the winter at home. The spring of 1926 we took on two jobs. One was crushing rock for the big mill that was being built at Lewiston. We crushed some two hundred thousand yards of rock for those works. Also they used our horses down there. The other contract that spring was building the road north out of Dayton for ten miles. Both these jobs lasted all that year and most of the next. Late in '27 we decided to quit construction work. By the time we got around to selling the construction equipment the nation was going into the depression and a number of the people that we'd sold to went through bankruptcy so we didn't ever get a lot of our money out of the equipment.

Going back now and filling in on the farming end of the business, in 1920 I bought what was called the Oliver Wilson place about a mile up Alkali Creek from Riparia. The most beautiful home in the country at that time was on that place. And I made the mistake of falling in love with the home and its setting and consequently paid about twice as much for it as I should have. However, I still continued to operate the McGregor place with my brother-in-law, Os Harvey, living there. In '24 McGregors decided to farm their own land and bought all the renters out. As far as the sheep business was concerned we continued to run sheep until the depression hit in 1930.

On February the sixth, 1924, I had a stroke of good luck when I married Lenora Harvey. Better known I guess as Auntie as she was a sister to May and an aunt to my three children. Our first baby died in October of '27 after a Cesarean operation. Then in May of 1929, the baby of the family, Della Mae came into the world.

I took my losses early in the depression years cutting down to fifteen hundred acres of pasture land around our home place with about forty acres under irrigation. So starting the depression years without any debts, six milk cows, four good kids and a hard-working wife as my most valuable assets along with friends and credits, I can truthfully say that the depression years were some of the happiest in my life. We probably ate better than we had before or since as we raised our own meat and had our cows and had a big garden which raised just a world of stuff. We had all we could possibly use from that garden and picked up more than our share of the cash by selling garden truck. Also we had quite a few fruit trees on the place so we had all the fruit we needed and then sold some besides. The rest of the irrigated land raised alfalfa for the stock so really I wished that everyone had eaten as good as we did through those times.

With the three older kids at the age when they should do things we devoted a lot of our leisure time doing things together. In the summer we did a lot of swimming in the river down at Riparia. I used to take the pickup with our kids and when we'd get into Riparia I'd let a yell out, "Let's go swimmin'," and at least twenty-five kids would pile on. When we'd get down to the river, Virginia, Scottie and Clay and several of the other kids would race to the far side of the river and back just for a warm up. We would have beach parties in the summer and then we'd sponsor dances in the winter at the school house. One dance in particular is well remembered not only by our own family but many other people, too. It was a big barbe-cue-dance, which had a record attendance of over five hundred. We had a ten-piece dance band, entertainers, electric lights and danced until daylight. We barbecued a whole steer, a pig and a lamb. We charged fifty cents admission and gave everyone all they could eat. We just broke even on the expenses. We had a lot of fun that night and have talked about it every once in awhile for years since. Besides dancing and swimming, our kids were particularly active in baseball and tennis. They put the little town of Riparia on the map with their sports.

The problem of education for the children came right in the mid-dle of the depression years. With Virginia it was one of the musts that she have some sort of a college degree as she was scholastically outstanding. She chose to go to Cheney Normal School. We let land go for taxes and with her picking up odd jobs we were able to keep her in college. With the boys it was different. I felt it was a choice of building property or an education. I knew we couldn't do both. With Clay it was not a problem, for from the first grade on it was a battle to get him to go to school. His teacher one day asked him what he was going to be when he got out of school and Clay said, "Grandpa."

In 1934 I found out what a blessing good health is when I broke my old back. This injury came as a result of arthritis growth in my spine which crystallized and when I received a severe jolt one of the vertebras was crushed. I spent what seemed like an endless time in the hospital. I was paralyzed from the waist down and it was a year before I could walk without help. From that time on it was a definite handicap that has ruled my life. For instance here just this past summer, Loretta, Virginia's youngest girl, asked her Grandmother if Grandpa was lazy because he wasn't mowing the lawn. Added to my own breakdown, Auntie had two serious cancer operations during the following two years.

In 1935 we added another member to our family when Virginia married Urgel Bell. In 1937 was another great milestone in my life when Linda, my first grandchild was born. Since then Urgel and Virginia have had three more girls—Lola, Lorna and Loretta.

All during these hard times by the family working together we were able to increase our holdings along Alkali Creek. We picked up contracts on several pieces of ground that fitted together until we had a block of land that had some four thousand acres of pasture land and twenty-five hundred of farm land. In 1938 our house burned so we felt that it would be more convenient to rebuild up on the farm land. We improved that place from an old homestead to a modern set of buildings. We farmed entirely with horses until 1940 when we traded them in on a tractor. The boys were grown and did nearly all the work themselves. By 1940 we had built up our cattle herd to around two hundred and fifty head. So all in all we had our work laid out for us.

However, our life wasn't entirely all work and no play during the late 30's and early 40's. In 1939 after the harvest was over seven of us piled into the pickup and took in the San Francisco World's Fair. And again in the fall of 1940 we went to the Fair in New York City and toured the East. Also, even though the boys were grown they had continued from little up to play baseball and they were some of the best players ever in the country. So every spring Sunday they would travel as much as a hundred miles to get to a ball game and Auntie and I would tag along to root for them.

We operated for several years as H.S. Barr and Sons until 1943 when I turned over the equipment and livestock to the boys and leased them the place. They continued the operations as Barr Brothers. Scottie was married to Evelyn Heimbigner that June of '43 and Auntie, Babe and I moved to Colfax for the following two years.

In 1944 Clay was married to Betty Flint and lived on another ranch at Washtucna. There were two sets of buildings on that place. Babe and I didn't like the city life of Colfax, mostly because old Doc Bryant had put Auntie to work as a nurse there in his clinic during the war. So we just sold the house and asked her if she wanted to move to Washtucna with us. We moved down there in September of 1945. While we were living there, Clay's and Betty's oldest girl, Carol was born. Later in 1950, Betty thrilled the whole family by giving birth to twins but then it was heartbreaking when the little boy died shortly afterward but leaving us little Mae. Up to 1952 I had been blessed with Granddaughters but it was that year that Clay and Betty saw fit to present me with my first Grandson, little Clay.

My youngest daughter, "Babe" was married in the fall of 1948 to Jim Beckner but that ended in tragedy when Jim was killed fourteen months later. We saw her through a rough period in her life and on into college. She spent two and a half years at Pullman then in 1954 she and Bill Evans were married and at the time of this writing Bill is in the army.

In the spring of '48 we bought a home in LaCrosse where we still live at the present time. In this last ten years I have called myself a retired farmer but actually I've had many interests all over the Northwest. One of them being a partner with a friend in a good apple orchard in the Yakima Valley. Also we've been interested in two big wheat ranches in Oreson and a cattle ranch in Montana. Also in this retired period of my life, Auntie and I've traveled throughout the United States, most of Canada and some of Mexico. Since the time Scottie moved from the old home place to Edwall in 1948, I have continued the operations of the ranch devoting most of my time to the management of that business.

Pop was a strong individual, with an exceptional woman at his side. He dictated his story in 1955. They lived in LaCrosse for the rest of his life. In 1959, he had a stroke, Mother took marvelous care of him at home for two years. He was born on January 2, 1879 and died on March 16, 1961.

A Tribute To Davy

by Della Evans

Over on the grade this spring there's been
    an eagle perched in Davy's tree.
The kids and grandkids really think
    it's marvelous to see.

That eagle showed up this year and
    everyone oohed and aahed with wonder
I kept still, but I knew
    and I didn't even ponder.

You see, years ago Davy
    had planted that lonely tree
And now, it's the only thing left
    from a man called Davy.

He had died before I was born
    but I knew him well
And this is a tribute to Davy
    that now I tell.

As I grew up I came to realize
    that man had left his mark—
For throughout our country was evidence
    of the work of this patriarch.

He was a carpenter
    of the finest kind
So that quality and Davy
    were synonymous in my mind.

When our country was being settled
    back in that early day
Lots of buildings were put up

just any old way.

But when someone wanted a building
    that was especially good
Davy was hired for his
    excellent craftsmanship was understood.

He built so many houses and barns
    around over our hills
That as I grew up there
    I knew about his many skills.

Now years have passed
    and a toil has been taken
At times it seems our hills
    have been forsaken.

Ranches were combined
    and folks moved to town
The Corp. of Engineers came along
    and Riparia was torn down.

The beautiful school closed
    that Davy had built—
It just seemed like there should have
    been some sort of guilt.

For sixty years I've watched as each
    of Davy's buildings went one by one.
Fire took a couple but mostly they seemed
    to vanish into oblivion.

Yet, one vacant barn lasted
    on the point of one high hill.
It acted as Davy's edifice
    or as a silent sentinel.

But last winter we had

a violent storm
And sure enough down went
        that one last barn
        and now I mourn.

Because Davy has certainly always
        been very real to me—
But now, standing there as a tombstone
        is that lonely tree.

So this spring when that
        beautiful eagle showed up
I couldn't help but quietly think—
        how very appropriate.

LENORA HARVEY BARR TORGESON

by Della Evans

I would like to include a short biographical sketch of my Mother as perhaps there are lessons here to be learned. I find it hard to write this biographical sketch as I have such vibrant memories of her. Lenora was really not a complicated person and if one term were to be used to describe her, it would be—caring.

That might be used to describe so much of her life. Her teen years were spent taking care of her ill mother. A short time after her mother's death, her sister became ill and Lenora cared for that sister's three children. That was a life-long commitment. The last two years of her husband Harvey's life, she nursed him night and day. Her entire life was a caring one.

Lenora was born to William Zane and Martha Jane Harvey in 1897. She has related many stories of her growing up years in the lower end of Whitman County in a book she wrote, called "Snake River Hills." Her early years were spent on homestead places in this area. Shortly after she got out of grade school, she went to San Francisco and Walla Walla with her sick mother.

After her mother's death she entered nurses training (which you could do then with just an eighth grade education). Then she set her sights higher and went to high school at Colfax, which she finished in two years and was accepted at Stanford University, where she wanted to go to law school.

Events have a way of changing a person's life and that happened to Lenora in 1923, when her older sister May died, leaving three little children. Lenora took those children and then married their father, Harvey Barr. She worked at his side for the rest of his life except for a brief two year period in the '40's when she worked for Dr. F.A. Bryant at the Bryant and Wiseman Clinic in Colfax.

When they married, Harvey was in the road construction business. They built many of the roads throughout the Pacific Northwest. At the same time as the construction business, they ran sheep, thousands of them.

They made two bad bids in 1927 that broke them and they sold out the construction equipment. The crash on Wall Street came in 1929. That set off the great depression and consequently, the Barrs never received payment on that equipment. Harvey and Lenora were forced to sell the sheep and range land back to creditors. This was an action that pulled them in to a home on Alkali Creek a mile from the little town of Riparia. They also had farm ground on the hills above.

Even though Lenora and Harvey didn't have very much at the beginning of the great depression of the '30's, they were better off than most of the country. We hope that we never again experience the throes of such times. The banks closed and folks lost all the money they had in banks. There were an awful lot of people after that who never trusted banks again even though there are now laws that protect your money. Everyone's main concern was merely getting food to the table. People living in cities were really in a bad way. Soup kitchens and bread lines were set up and this was how millions survived. Harvey, in later life said they were more fortunate than most. They lived and worked hard together and from the beginning of the depression they made gains. They had fruit trees, a big garden, sold cream, butchered hogs and turkeys, all for cash. They had land and there raised some wheat and cattle. To get cattle Harvey and Lenora went to Genessee, Idaho and bought a cattle-car load for $14.00 a head in 1934. So they found ways to survive. One very helpful foot-up was a thousand dollars that Lenora inherited which she buried in a fruit jar. Lenora drove school kids which brought in a monthly check. Another cash income was boarders she kept. One set of boarders was a crew of surveyors that was the first step for all the dams that later were built on the Snake River. Everyone worked hard in those days but there were choices that had to be made. Mortgage companies held more property than did individuals. So it was then that the Barrs picked up farming ground for very cheap prices.

Even though Lenora and Harvey worked hard, they also played. Tennis was popular and the three older children were all good athletes and excelled at tennis. The boys played baseball and the whole family went to watch. There was swimming in the Snake River in the summer and dances to attend in the winter, so the hard working family did play. No television! A lot of card games were played around those kerosene lamps in the evenings.

Lenora was certainly a force throughout those times. It was during those hard times of the thirties that Harvey broke his back, then a year later she discovered a lump in her breast. Her mother had died of breast cancer so she knew the implications. Remember this was the mid-thirties and medical technology was not what it is today. They did operate, a complete mastectomy one side, then a year later, the other and the next year, radium treatments of cancer in the uterus. She was a survivor.

By 1938, they had farm land up on the hill above their home on Alkali, so when the house caught fire, they moved up there. Times continued to improve. They bought more farm ground, prices were better and both Lenora's and Harvey's health had improved. Even though they worked hard, it was better. The oldest daughter, Virginia was married and lived over the hill so Lenora kept the oldest granddaughter while Virginia taught school at Riparia. The family went to San Francisco to the World's Fair in 1939 and in 1940, a trip to New York Fair and throughout the east.

The second World War hit in 1941. While shortages made farming difficult, prices for wheat and cattle improved. The financial picture was so much better for the Barr family. Other aspects of their lives were also good. Electricity came by the Rural Electrification Act that brought far-reaching electric lines. The Barrs got rid of all those work horses and bought a tractor in 1939. In 1940, they bought a new Chevrolet sedan for $600.00 and paid cash for it.

In 1943, their oldest son, Scott married and since I had just finished grade school, Harvey and Lenora leased the ranch to their sons and moved to Colfax. There they bought a lovely home for $5,000.00.

This was at the height of World War II and everyone was involved with the war effort. Lenora, a trained nurse, met her doctor on the street just shortly after moving into Colfax. He said, "Lenora, everyone is being drafted these days. Report to work tomorrow morning." Young nurses were away in the service so all available nurses were needed. Lenora worked twelve hour shifts; most of the time as a nursery nurse with the many babies that were being born then. She enjoyed her work and made many friends.

However, in 1945, the boys had bought a ranch at Washtucna that had an extra house on it. So they moved to that ranch where they lived until 1948.

When the war came to a close so that Harvey and Lenora, like all the country, could get on with their personal lives and their own desires, the Barrs enjoyed travel and immediately went east.

In 1948, the boys broke up their partnership. Scott moved to Edwall and Clay took over the Washtucna place, thus turning the ranch back to Harvey and Lenora. Rather than move back to the hills they bought a home in LaCrosse. They continued to take trips and spent a couple winters in Arizona.

Then in 1959, Harvey suffered a stroke, Lenora hired some help and kept him at home until he passed away in 1961.

Lenora's health should be reviewed, but more important was her attitude and how she coped. As mentioned, she had radical surgeries in the '30's. In the '50's she seemed to contact pneumonia so easily, then gall bladder problems and surgery and again a hysterectomy surgery in the early '60's. Probably though, the most serious illness was in 1958, when she became so ill, the doctors sent her to the Mayo Clinic in Minnesota; there they diagnosed meningitis-encephalitis. However, her attitude was always that of a fighter and she would be right back on her feet, never feeling sorry for herself. Even later she developed diveruticulitis and would be incredibly sick one day and out playing bridge the next. Her attitude was always, if someone said go, she'd say, I'm ready.

In 1963, she married Ted Torgeson and they went on a two month trip to Europe. They continued to live in LaCrosse, taking many more trips; another one to Europe; to Hawaii; to South America; to Canada; various places in the United States and four winters in Arizona. They sold their big house and moved into a double-wide trailer where they were very comfortable. Lenora's joys of being close to family and her friends remained of utmost importance to her right to the end of her eighty-seven years of a very full life.

A STORY

by Yvonne LaRae Hoffman

God blew a big breath.
And there was some clay there.
God breathed into the clay
And the clay became a man.
The breath inside the man was a soul.
The man breathed in and out.
His breath mingled with the breath
Of all the living things that God had made.
The mingled breath became the soul of the world.
And when death came to the world
The world's last, long breath returned to God.
God breathed it in and all again became Him.

HOWDY GAL!

by Ralph E. Morgan

Howdy Gal!

I hears yer a hankerin' fer a good, strong man. Shucks ma'am don't ya be lookin' any furthur, I am here. Utah is whats folks calls em, but I reckons I'l jes' 'bout answers to anythin' long's ya don't git carried too fer aways. I reckon y'll wonders how come I gits yer addressee, well, my ol' pardner "Morg," he fixed me up with it and sez you'd be awaitin' to git muh writin'. Well, ma'am, I gots to tell ya, I ain't had much of that book larnin', but I kin spel purty good.

Yep, ma'am, I came clear up frum Utah country jest so we kin gits hitched. Muh ol' pardner sez that's yur a right good woman. . . a farmin' gal the ways I hears it. Them good-lookin' farm gals is hard to comes by I reckon. The ways I hears it told, you been a gittin' some of that book larnin' and I was plumb-tickled to hears that cuz now theres gonna be edjeekated folks, I reckons we kin fetch up sum purty brite youn'uns. Yep, I'll be purty proud to be teamed up with sech a outstandin' person as yerself. I also heared it told thats y'll a rite fine cookin' gal whose purty good at makin' her own clothes, by cracky, I shor can't wait to meet ta. Jest hold on a minut ma'am, Morg, he shoutin' sumpthin at me. wel, shucks ma'am, ain't taht 'bout the bes' news ever. . . he sez ya gots all yer teeth too, by gollly. . . I reckons yer a rite fine woman.

Ol' Bessie and me will comes over thar and see ya at that larnin' place one of these here days. Don't ya be frettin' any none ma'am, Bessie, she's muh horse. yep, we rode many a trail together, ma'am, ol' Bessie the best frien' I evers had, shor hope ya takes a likkin' to her ma'am, cuz I reckons we can't be agittin' hitched if'n ya don't likks ol' Bessie. I 'member the winter back in '68, ma'am, shor was a mean one, I hear it told that yuh folks git yer share of snow up thisaways. . . anyways ma'am, I kin 'member many a nite ol' Bess and me wood sits aroun' that fire. . . only one thing 'bout ol' Bess, ma'am, she warn't never much at talkin'.

Shucks ma'am, I reckon I 'bout chewed yer ear off with all this talkin', I gits wond up purty good sum times. Y'll keeps yer lamp burnin' fer me ma'am so I kin gits to the rite room. Shucks, ma'am, I shor am glad to meet ya, muh al' ranch will be rite proud to have ya, course y'll have to be fixin' up the place jest a mite, we gots runnin' water too ma'am and next year after we gits those cattle to market, I'll have that man in town fix ya up with sum of them new fangled lits that don't needs no oil or nothin', ya jest turn a lil' ol' nobbie and that ol' thang glows rite brite. I heard tell 'bout sum folks in the next county thats gots a inside john. Wal, ma'am, I reckon sumbody is jest a pullin' muh leg. . . who ever heard of such a thang. . . why everybody knows one of them thar outbuildin's wood never fit inside a house. Them folks must think I ain't had no larnin', well, I guess I showed 'em, huh? I'm a purty slick fella when I haves to be, course, ma'am, I'd never use none of them fancy tricks on you. Wal, ma'am, I reckon I better be afixin' one of them thar stampies on this here letter so as the ol' boy down the road kin picks it up. Y'll take care of yerself, ma'am, and 'member to puts in a good word fer me when ya sez yer prayers tonite. I'll be awaitin' to hear frum ya, ma'am.

Bye fer now.
Love. . .Utah Schultz

WHO WILL MARRY THE MERRY PRINCESS MARYBELL?

by Steve Kenworthy

Once upon a merry time, there lived upon a merry hill
A merry king, a merry queen, and their merry daughter, MaryBell.
Now, MaryBell was a merry maid, and fair beside the fact
But her merry parents were not very for the one thing that she
    lacked—
A merry husband, a merry prince, the merry princess could not reap.
Although wealth and beauty she guarded well, her temper she could
    not keep.
The merry rumor spread far and wide that lived within this land
A merry maid, fair in fact, that to a prince would give her hand.

And so each morning to the castle door came a merry knock—
Another prince from a far off land had come to bid wedlock.
And when the merry lads had seen the princess they'd come to wed
Their merry hearts within them leaped: they found true what had
    been said.
The anxious lads would merry court, and with merry words their
    love expound
But if they did just one thing wrong, her merry wrath they merry
    found.
And so, come they came and go they went, the royal lads without a
    hitch
For they all knew that beauty was nothing if the princess wasn't
    very nice.

Within the merry castle walls the merry king lamented
And to his merry royal queen his merry sorrows vented.
"What can we do? What can we do? My kingdom is on the line!"
Replied the merry queen to him, "Relax, and hear this thought of
    mine.
"We've looked and searched and merry begged for a prince to marry
    her

When the answer's plain—to marry a bitch we need a merry cur.
So let us search, instead a prince, a man who's merry mean."
A merry smile creased the merry king's face. This answer he had not
    seen.

And so the merry king sent forth from his merry presence
a merry herald and proclamation to his merry peasants.
And this the merry message said a prince's shoes would fill
He who had the courage to marry the merry princess, MaryBell.
And so the merry subjects came from throughout the merry land—
The tall, the short, the weak, the strong—to bid the maiden's hand.
But none were found to meet the need; the herald's anxiety grew.
And then a voice deep within the crowd said, "I will marry the
    shrew."

The merry crowd quickly spread, the man who spoke stood all
    alone.
The merry whispers flew merry fast. It was the man called Harry
    Stone.
The merry herald knew at once that before him stood the man
Who could merry solve the merry woes of the king to whom he ran.
"I've found the lad, the merry lad, your daughter for to marry!
He's mean they say—a merry cur—but the folks just call him
    Harry."
The merry king couldn't believe his ears; a merry victory he had
    won!
The merry marriage began right then, by night he had a son.

And so the new found merry prince departed with his merry bride.
They went to a nearby mountain top, there a honeymoon to abide.
But it was not merry long until the merry villagers could hear
A sound that grew, and grew, and grew 'til they were filled with fear.
At first they did not know what it was and sent one to discover.
The merry news was that is was a merry princess and her lover.
For forty days and forty nights the merry rumble went non-stop.
The shouts and screams and merry shrieks hailed down from on the
    mountain top.

And then one merry morning heard the merry villagers below
A merry silence—no sound at all—what happened they did not
    know.
So merry quiet was all the land that whispers they could hear.
From on the mountain top one said "I love you," the other "I love
    you, too, my dear."
And then exploded merry glee in every corner of the land
The subjects merry cheered for him to whom the princess gave her
    hand.
Merry soon the merry couple came from off their mountain top
To start their merry reign amidst the merry cheers that wouldn't
    stop.

Forever merry lived the couple and their children numbered seven,
But this the merry couple learned—you go through hell to get to
    heaven.

THAT WAS THE YEAR

by Edith Erickson

Author's note: This manuscript combines things I found while researching for Colfax: 100 Plus. *Some occurred in 1910, some 1948, and some in 1963. The old man in the story was my grandfather.*

—*Edith E. Erickson*

November had been rainy. The rivers and creeks in the whole area were running full. December became cold and snowy. The already full rivers froze quickly and soon were covered with at least a foot of ice. Snow was several feet deep everywhere. At times when the wind blew transportation of all kinds was brought to a complete halt. Trains, buses, and even snow plows had trouble moving. On most residential streets the snow was pushed so high along the edges of the yards that people could not see across the streets. Roofs often had to be shoveled because of the weight of the snow. The storm drains all over town were covered with ice and snow. The streets were a glare of ice. In fact, the whole town was a mess. Meetings were canceled, some days schools were closed. Everyone was praying for a break in the weather.

When the schools were closed, how the children enjoyed coasting, skating and making snowmen and forts. It was the best snow that many of them had ever seen.

January came with wind moving the snow into huge drifts and completely baring the ground in others, thus making those areas freeze deeper and deeper. The temperature continued just enough below freezing that no thawing could occur. As the end of the month came into sight the weather suddenly changed. In the early evening a Chinook wind began to blow and a heavy rain moved into the area and began to melt the snow.

In just a few hours water was everywhere. Sirens blew loud and long. Nearly every able bodied man and many women rushed down town to see what the emergency was. As they opened their doors they were greeted by very brisk winds, rain, and water running every where.

Not only were most of the storm drains covered with snow and ice, but the few that were open had ice blocks in the pipes leading from them to the river or the sewer pond. Water ran on top of the ice. It soon ran over the roads and down the streets. Not long it was up to the edges of the sidewalks. Shop keepers rushed to sandbag where ever possible. The water from the east hill surged not only down the top of the creek but tore the bared rocks from the top of the hill carrying them all the way to the Main Street. The water rushed through the basement of a church as a rock crushed the window and the force of the water swung the door open. The whole north end of town was a rising lake. Slush moved on the south part of Main Street.

By 3 a.m. people in boats began to check all lowland houses where they knew elderly or people with problems lived. In one house on North Main Street they found a ninety year old man and his eighty year old wife standing barefoot in several inches of water. He had his pants rolled up to his knees and they both held their shoes and stockings in their hands as they stood watching the water inch higher and higher in their kitchen. The rescuers wanted to carry them out, but they were very independent old people and insisted on walking out to the edge of their water covered porch where they were helped into a boat and transported to a place where they could be transferred into a car and taken to the safety of his sister's house, which was much higher on the hill.

A fire was found burning in the basement of a chemical warehouse. Nothing was done about it. The water had caused the chemical to ignite and the bags above the water level were burning briskly. The warehouse was located in such a way the men felt the bags would soon be under water so the fire could cause no serious damage.

The ice began to break up. The noise was terrific. Huge chunks began to move. Bridges were in danger of being damaged or even destroyed. The golf course became a mountain of ice with the big moving chunks digging deep holes into the ground.

Some of the braver men went for explosives. With danger to themselves the men planted the sticks of dynamite as far from the banks of the river as they dared to go out on the shifting ice. They hoped to break up the largest chunks so that it would move quickly and safely under the bridges.

When day light came a few people on the far north end of town were found stranded on the second floor of their houses where they had peacefully slept through the storm and had not wakened until the ice in the river near them began to break up and move around. They lived too far from the center of town to hear the sirens that had blown at the fire stations.

By mid morning the wind had subsided and the rain had slackened. The worst of the storm was over. It seemed as if all of the lower parts of town were afloat. There was not only water in many of the homes but six churches had water in their buildings, the courthouse, two schools and most of the stores were also damaged. The only way to travel Main Street was in a boat.

Electricity was out. Only those people with battery radios were able to learn of the wide spread damage that had been done in the surrounding country and in town. Hundreds and hundreds of acres were under water. Millions of dollars worth of damage had been done but no lives in the area had been lost.

It was weeks before the town was back to normal. For some people it was never normal again as some houses and places of business were completely destroyed by the terrible rush of water. The waves damaged walls of a new house on a basement. The walls washed out and the house dropped to the bottom.

After the old man that was rescued had had some sleep he stood at the window of his sister's house and looked down on the acres and acres of water below him. He took his wife's and his sister's hands and said, "Let us all repeat the 23rd Psalm" so together they said

The Lord is my shepherd, I shall not want.
He maketh me to lie down in green pasture.
He leadeth me beside the still water.
He restoreth my soul.
He leadeth me in the paths of righteousness for his name sake.
Yea, though I walk through the valley of the shadow of death
I will fear no evil for thou art with me;
Thy rod and thy staff they comfort me
Thou preparest a table before me
in the presence of mine enemies;

Thou anointest my head with oil;
My cup runneth over
Surely goodness and mercy shall follow me
all the days of my life and
I will dwell in the house of the Lord forever.

At the close he said, "That Psalm is as true now as when David wrote it so many, many years ago. We have so much to be thankful for.

As for the old man and his wife, they soon were back into their house. Neighbors and family came to their rescue and cleaned the mud and debris from the main part of the house and made it as livable as before. The basement forever and ever smelled musty and was more or less unusable. Their yard was covered with coal that had been carried from the coal yard a few blocks away. Since they had a coal burning stove to heat the house little by little all the little chunks of coal was gathered and disposed of.

In spite of his age and the damage done to his home he still had a keen sense of humor. To members of his family he wrote, "Any person who is an adept swimmer can find plenty of houses for sale. Do not go to a real estate man to find a well furnished house. You can just see the owner and save the commission."

As things gradually dried out and the grass began to peak through the thick layer of mud the old man often stood on the porch and said. "Truly, truly, the Lord is our Shepherd."

JOGGING SCENE

by Jeff Lageson

Step. Step. Step.
Plod.
Left right. Left right.
Pant. Pant. Pant.
Avoid hurl.
Cough. Spit.
Talk about things.
Nod. Keep up with buddy.

EIGHT BLUE SNAKES

by Karen Kenworthy

Hi, my name is Susan. I like to be called Sue, but just about everyone calls me Susie. I really don't mind being called Susie, but now that I'm eleven years old, I think Sue sounds more to my age. Mom said I was just being silly when I told her that. When I said that it wasn't like I was asking her to call me a whole new name she said she would try, but that habit can be hard to break.

My mom's name is Helen and people say she can cook anything. I never thought much about it until I was old enough to start having sleep-overs with my best friend Tasha. I love Tasha's mom a lot, and she has always been real sweet to me. Mom has said many times that she is glad Tasha and I are friends. But Tasha's mom doesn't cook. She opens cans, she opens boxes, and she can use the microwave, but she doesn't cook.

I would try to be polite and eat whatever was given to me just like my mom had said, but I think Mrs. Alred figured out that I didn't really care for her meals because now when I go over she gets pizza or chicken. I can eat boxed macaroni and cheese, but it sure doesn't taste anything like Mom's homemade kind with chunks of cheese and ham in it. Breakfast was always better at Tasha's though. At our house breakfast is always mush. Oat mush, corn mush, cracked wheat mush, and four grain mush. Tasha's mom always has cold cereal. Not just Cherrios and Rice Chex, but Froot Loops, Captain Crunch and all the ones Mom says we can't afford or have too much sugar in them. Fred would always be jealous when he found out that I got to have the yummy cereal.

Fred's my little brother. He's six years old. I asked Mom once why there was so many years between us. She said it just worked out that way. That's the kind of answer I always get when she's real busy. Fred's not a bad kid, for a brother. He's always getting into trouble, which makes me look good. I like to tease him and he loves to try and pull pranks on me. I'm usually too smart to let him get me though. Maybe because he's five years younger than me, I am more patient with him than some of my friends are with their little brothers and sisters. Fred and I couldn't be more different about most things. We don't like the same TV programs, music, games or just about anything. When I complain that he never wants to do what I want to do, Mom says that five years makes a big difference. When I was his age I liked his music and programs too. I guess she's right, but it can get frustrating sometimes.

One thing everyone agrees on though, is that we are brother and sister. We look much the same. I don't look like a boy or anything, but we both have strawberry-blonde hair, blue eyes and the slightest hint of freckles on our faces. I have always hated the freckle thing, but Mom assured me that as I grow, they will disappear. She would have me watch the *Ann of Green Gables* movies to show me that I had it even better than her and things had worked out. She would always say that women paid lots of money to try and get this color of hair. I didn't really care. In the summer I would try and stay out in the sun so it would bleach to more blonde than strawberry, but I would burn like crazy and Mom would get mad at me for being so foolish.

I have often wondered if Mom was ever my age. She is tall and I am getting tall too. I have been hoping that I slow down soon because Tasha is a small, petite girl and I feel big and clumsy next to her. I think it's more lady like to be pretty and small. Mom says it's nice to be different and someday, if I am lucky like her, I'll find someone who will love me for who I am like Dad loves her. I don't know why Dad wouldn't love her. She is very talented and can be funny when she wants to. Mostly, she's always been there for us. Mom says she should stop eating so much of her own cooking. Dad always gives her a big hug and says "I like ya fat 'n' sassy". I figure they're just teasing around because Mom looks just fine to me. She looks like . . . a mother.

We live in a nice three bedroom house in Orem, Utah. Our back-yard isn't real big, but Dad likes it that way. ("Low maintenance," he says.) Mom loves her kitchen because it's pretty big and has lots of counter space, but most of all it has a good dishwasher. We have the kitchen, the three bedrooms, a family room and a nice bathroom on the main floor. In the basement we have a another big room we call the den and a big unfinished part we use for storage. Dad keeps saying that one of these days he's going to put a full bathroom down there. Mom just sighs and doesn't say anything. I would like a bathroom down there, but I also love having the unfinished part to play in when its winter time and too cold to play outside. Mom loves having the storage area for food storage. When something is on sale at the grocery store she buys at least one case and then I have to help Dad haul it down to the basement.

It seems like it's always my job to clean the basement. I hate doing the corners of the storeroom. Spider webs just seem to pop out of no where. That always gives me the creeps. Sometimes I can get Fred to come down and do that part because the spiders don't bother him.

So, that's where I am. Down in the basement. I'm to dust the food storage and vacuum the den. I just found something that I haven't seen in several months. I guess that means I haven't been doing such a great job cleaning lately. I found a blue rubber snake. Fred had been collecting them for months. Every time his kindergarten teacher would let him pick out of the prize box, he would feel around until he felt a snake and then pull it out. By the time school was out for the year he had eight of them. They were blue, about 6 inches long, and you could almost see through them, but Fred loved his snakes.

All summer Fred would try and scare people with his eight rubber snakes. Sometimes Mom would get mad because Fred would put them in the kitchen. One time Fred taped a blue snake to the phone handle. When Mom answered the phone, she felt the yucky rubber snake and screamed as she dropped the phone. Fred ran over and picked up the phone to ask who was calling. It was Dad! Fred's expression turned from mischievous to worried. He was sure he was in for it now. Dad asked what had happened. As he explained, Fred's worried face turned into a grin as he heard Dad begin to laugh. Mom just rolled her eyes and walked off to get a drink of water. Fred could usually make Dad laugh. Mom would always tell him to stop encouraging Fred, but dad just couldn't help himself.

Those eight blue snakes would show up just about anywhere, any time. It was amazing how creative Fred could get with his pranks. One time Fred even scared me, his sweet sister Sue. I thought I was too smart to be caught by one of his silly tricks, but I was wrong.

I laid my clean clothes on my bed. Nothing fancy, just a pair of jeans and a pink tee-shirt. Then I went off to take a shower. I must admit that I goofed around a while because no one was waiting to use the shower. After I blow-dried my hair, I went into my room to get dressed. I pulled on my shirt and then put on my socks. I always put my socks on before my pants. I don't know why, I just do. So then I slipped into my jeans and pulled them up. After I snapped and zipped them I shoved my hands into my pockets, to make sure they lay flat and weren't sticking out. That's what did it! I started hopping around tying to strip my pants off and yelling "Oh, gross! Oh, gross!" It felt like I had a slug or fat worm in my pocket. It was slimy and . . . GROSS!!

I was yelling for mother, and just about had my pants off when the door opened and there was Fred laughing his head off, and pointing at me. I suddenly realized I'd been had. My stupid little brother and one of his blue rubber snakes had caught up with me. I hiked up my pants and made a run for the door. Fred giggled and started to run down the hall. If my mom hadn't shown up right then I was going to catch Fred and make him eat his stupid blue snake. But Mom grabbed us both and demanded to know what was going on. I reached once more into my pocket and produced a slimy blue rubber snake for my mother's inspection.

"What have you been doing Frederick Alexander?!" my mother scolded, cringing as I passed her Fred's snake. "And what on earth have you done to it to make it so slimy and . . . well . . . gross!" my mother asked disgusted and bewildered.

Fred straightened up and had a look on his face like a Cheshire cat. He looked as though he was about to bless us with a key to something very special. "I slathered it in Vaseline, isn't that great! I thought it up last night, and I could hardly sleep thinking about doing it this morning. You know the really hard part was getting it into Sue's pocket without getting Vaseline all over the top of the pocket. You know what I did, I just took . . ."

"That's quite enough young man, now off to your room while I think this out," Mom said, cutting off Fred's excited explanation."

My humor and genius are lost on this family. Dad's the only one who seems to understand me," Fred mumbled as he went off to his room.

Mom then turned to me and asked if I had more clean pants. I told her I did and turned to go back to my room. She assured me that Fred would get a fitting punishment, and that I still needed to love him even though he could be a pest at times. I just gave her one of my best put-upon looks and headed back up the hall. As I walked I wasn't sure, but I thought I heard my mom whisper under her breath "He's just like his dad."

I must say I was surprised when I heard what kind of punishment my mom had come up with for Fred. Usually it was the same old thing. Either sit in the corner for 15 minutes, grounded for a day or two, or if we did something really bad, a spanking.

I must admit that getting a spanking took a little getting used to. When we first realized that only Dad's spankings really hurt we would almost laugh when mom would try. She'd be all mad, or as she would put it " very disappointed," and take us in the den and try giving us a good spanking. She would get so worked up and we would brace ourselves, and then . . . nothing. If her hand hurt as much as she said, then she got it worse than us. When Mom would realize that we were happy it didn't hurt, she would get even madder. Then she would find something else to spank us with to get the point across. We learned to show enough pain to make Mom satisfied that she had done a proper job. We did feel bad about what we had done. Just to see Mom that mad would be enough for me anyway.

So, when I heard about Mom's new solution I was surprised. There was Fred at the sink with my jeans. Mom was explaining to him how to get all the Vaseline out of the pocket before it could be put in the washing machine. Mom turned to me as she noticed me in the room and told me that the punishment would fit the crime. Fred would be having an in-depth lesson on doing the laundry.

I was a little skeptical because that meant Mom had to follow Fred around to make sure the job got done. Mom was always so busy, I wondered how much she would follow through. Oh well. Fred looked fairly miserable. That was good enough for me. It took him a long time to wash out those pants. When Fred brought me a load of clothes including my jeans he had yucked up, he looked very bored and I had to smile at his repentant attitude.

Since that time I haven't seen much of his rubber snakes. I guess its been enough time that thinking about it makes me laugh. He hasn't given up on the pranks and tricks, though, thinking the whole world thinks he's funny, but I know he has a new respect for Vaseline.

CHRISTMAS IS . . .

by Jennifer Lee Wigen (age 14)

Christmas is a
Holiday for
Rejoicing
In the birth of our
Savior, it is also a
Time to be
Merry
And think of everybody as being
Special.

GRANDPA JOE AND
THE ANGEL OF THE LORD

by Alisa M. Largent

My Grandpa Joe loved a stretcher better'n anyone, his own and the old favorites like Paul Bunyan and Babe the Blue Ox. Although I'm still a mite young to be a proper storyteller, I try to keep up the tradition now that he's gone. So pull up a rocker and grab yourself a whittlin' stick, but mind, don't slice your thumb on that jackknife; you city folks ain't too handy with such things. Comfy? Well, then, I've just the yarn to spin as we keep comp'ny today. It's about Grandpa Joe and the angel of the Lord.

Now, Grandpa Joe was always an ornery cuss. There are more tales on him than ticks on a hound in July. Like the time he was in grade school and him and a buddy snuck a goat into the school at night. They put it right on the teacher's desk. Next morning that goat was still there, standing as pretty as you please on the desk. It had eaten off all the papers . . . and left a few offerings of its own instead.

Grandpa didn't get any better as he got older. There was the time my momma was in high school and was having a slumber party. She was all in a tizzy trying to make refreshments, welcome her guests and do whatever else needs to be done for slumber parties. Anyway, it is obvious she wasn't thinking clear because when Grandpa offered to make the sandwiches, she let him. Normally, she would have been suspicious. He set right to work, doing a nice job on those sandwiches. He cut them in half and served them all stacked up on a plate. The way Momma tells it, they were great sandwiches. All the girls thought so—until they were finished and Grandpa Joe told them the sandwiches were made from canned dog food.

Well, like I said, Grandpa Joe was always an ornery cuss, but never more so than when he died. It happened in the summer. The day was terrible hot; TV and radio weathermen were telling everyone to stay inside where it was cool. Grandpa was never one for sitting still or taking orders, so he decided to mow the grass. If you already guessed he had a heart attack, you are right.

Grandpa Joe was dead before the ambulance got there. The ambulance team worked on him, but it wasn't any use. They finally left us alone to make arrangements for the funeral. It was a miserable day.

My daddy called the funeral home. The owner, Mr. Taylor, was a personal friend of the family. Grandma has some old-fashioned ways and wanted Grandpa Joe laid out in the parlor, so Mr. Taylor agreed to bring over the casket and fix Grandpa up at home. Everything went along normally, if anything can be normal at a time like that, until Mr. Taylor put Grandpa in the casket.

The first inkling we had of trouble was when Mr. Taylor stepped into the hall from the parlor and shut the door quickly behind himself. He was very calm as he asked my daddy to come with him for just a moment. Daddy looked puzzled, but followed Mr. Taylor into Grandma's parlor.

I was itchy to know what was happening and would have listened at the door if my momma hadn't-a been with me. After what was pretty near forever, Daddy came out. He seemed exasperated. He kept rubbing the back of his neck and sticking his hands in his pockets. Momma asked what was wrong. He hemmed and hawed and looked out the front window and rubbed the back of his neck. Finally, he said he should have expected something like this from Grandpa Joe, but he hadn't. Daddy thought Grandpa would at least behave for his own funeral. But the fact of the matter was . . . Grandpa was sitting up in his casket refusing to be buried. Not that he wasn't dead. He was just flat refusing to be buried.

My momma sighed. She said it was hard enough on Grandma and the rest of us now without him playing these games. We went upstairs to tell Grandma the news. She rolled her eyes to the ceiling and declared "that's just like Joe."

We all went into the parlor to see Grandpa Joe. Daddy was right. Grandpa was sitting up in the casket giving Mr. Taylor what-for for trying to bury a spring chicken like himself before his time. Grandma broke in and told him to quit badgering Mr. Taylor, he was just doing his job. After all, Grandpa was dead and somebody needed to get him ready. He shouldn't be so ungrateful.

Grandpa wasn't to be shushed. He said he was in the prime of his life. What were we about, putting him away at such an early age? Daddy explained that he had had a heart attack and was dead, but Grandpa Joe snorted and declared that to be hogwash. A man didn't die from mowing the grass. He ought to know, he'd been mowing the grass since he was seven years old, and not with some fancy-pants sit-down mower either, no sir. He'd used a push mower up until his fifties, when Daddy bought him that electric start. Healthy as a horse, he was. Didn't need no casket, that's for darn sure.

You can, perhaps, appreciate the situation we were in. Momma had already called kin to come for the funeral. Neighbors would be stopping by to bring food. I thought we could hold them off from going into the parlor that night, but it would be difficult to have a proper viewing the next day with the body sitting up and talking to the visitors. It just wasn't done.

Since we wouldn't let Grandpa Joe leave the parlor, he insisted we bring in the TV so-as he could watch the Reds game. We held a family conference in the kitchen to map out some strategy. Grandpa interrupted us once, hollering for a Coke and potato chips. He was right irate to find we were out and said he would go to the store himself and get some. Mr. Taylor hastily volunteered to go instead.

We all agreed that Grandpa Joe knew he was dead and was just being ornery in not lying down. The problem was getting him to admit it and then cooperate.

We decided Grandma should be the first to try her hand. She went into the parlor and scolded Grandpa Joe, just as she had her whole married life. She told him that enough was enough; he'd had his day for playing pranks and now it was time to give them up. Lord knows, it wasn't going to be easy for her without him, but all life came to an end. If she could face up to that, then so should he.

I don't know if something Grandma said gave him the idea or if he thunk it up on his own, but Grandpa decided to devil her for a spell. He asked her how come she was so anxious to have him dead. He said he didn't have no money to speak of, so it couldn't be that. Maybe she had some young buck on the sly that was waiting to slip into his shoes. You should-a heard Grandma spit and sputter about that.

Grandpa Joe started speculatin' about the different men in the neighborhood, wondering which one would call on Grandma after a respectable time had elapsed. At least, he said, he did hope she'd wait a respectable time. Otherwise she would get a very bad reputation. Grandma was furious by this time. The only thing she managed to say was, "Oh, Joe!", then she turned on her heel and stomped out of the parlor. You could hear Grandpa's big belly laugh halfway down the street.

Momma didn't want to talk to Grandpa Joe by herself, so she and Daddy went in together. My daddy prided himself on how well he kept control, and I could tell he was trying to make this a calm and serious discussion. He should-a known better. First thing, Grandpa asked it they knew which one of the men Grandma was going to replace him with. That made Momma mad and wore off some of the calm early in the discussion. Then Grandpa Joe said he'd been doing some figuring, and being dead wasn't such a bad deal after all. If Daddy notified the IRS that Grandpa was dead, but didn't notify the bank or GTE, maybe he could draw retirement but not have to pay taxes. Daddy sighed. I don't think the conversation was going as he had planned. It was a good thing Mr. Taylor returned right then with Grandpa's Coke and chips.

I was the last one to go in the parlor. Grandpa Joe fixed me with a stare and asked if I was going to start in on him, too. I said no, but I did have one question. Wasn't he going to smell in a couple of days? He laughed and laughed and said probably not any worse than usual. Then he offered me some potato chips and I sat down to watch the game with him.

Mr. Taylor left. The rest of us hung around, trying to do normal things, not saying much. We went to bed with Grandpa's TV still sounding from the parlor. How in the world were we going to get him to lie down? I woke up with that same question on my mind. But, as it turned out, I needn't have worried. Something happened during the night that changed Grandpa's mind for us.

Grandpa Joe was a different man the next morning. He was, well, meek is the way my daddy put it. Ashamed of himself. No sign of mischief anywhere. He said an angel of the Lord visited him in the night. The angel wanted to know why he was refusing his call to go home. The angel also wanted to know if Grandpa Joe was mighty enough to turn his back upon the Lord and not suffer the consequences. He told Grandpa it was time to make amends to his family and come along.

This angel must have made a powerful impression on Grandpa because, as I said, he was a changed man. Still sitting in his casket, he kissed each of us good-bye and said he was sorry for the trouble he'd caused. He held Grandma extra-special close, which brought tears to everyone's eyes. Then, giving us all one last look, he lay back in his casket and pulled the top closed.

It was a few minutes before anyone could move. Momma and Grandma were crying. I felt kind of numb, now it was all over. Daddy was the first to go to the casket. He stretched out his hand and bent his knees, like he was going to kneel and pray. Just as his hand touched the casket, a familiar voice shouted, "Gotcha!". I never saw my daddy jump so high in his life—and backwards, too. We listened to Grandpa Joe's deep belly laugh from inside the casket, loud at first, then fading away. I looked around and everyone was smiling. Grandma said, "That's just like Joe."

Well, that's my story. It's not near as good as the ones Grandpa used to tell. I sure miss that old man. But if I know Grandpa, which I do, and if I were a gamblin' man, which I'm not, I'd bet Grandpa was hanging around the top steps of the Golden Gate about now, swappin' stretchers with the angel of the Lord.

CHRISTMAS IS COMING

by Jennifer Lee Wigen (age 14)

Christmas is coming I can feel it in my bones
Baby Jesus is sleeping without a moan.

Christmas is coming I can tell by the smell
Gingerbread boys as big as a church bell

Christmas is coming I can tell by the sights
The houses are so very bright.

Christmas is coming I can tell by the taste
Cookies are never put to waste.

Christmas is coming I can hear it all around
Carolers singing sweet songs all through the town.

TAMMY AND SANDY

by Alysia Herr (age 7)

Once upon a time there was a turtle named Sandy. It was her first day of school. But she was shy. None of the other turtles would play with her. So all that day she had no one to play with. It went on and on. Then one day there was a new turtle in the class. The turtle's name was Tammy. Tammy had no one to play with either. Then one day Tammy met Sandy. They said "Hi" to each other. Then Sandy said, "Do you want to play on the tires?" "Sure," said Tammy. So they went out to recess and got on the tires. Tammy pushed first. They let other turtles on. The kids thanked them. Then they were all friends. The end.

A NEW DAY

by Yvonne LaRae Hoffman

Long, blue shadows
Fall across the lawn.
Fingers of sunlight
Proclaim the coming dawn.

The tall trees stand
Bathed in jeweled light;
Each single leaf
A dewy, shining bright.

Closed sleeping flowers
open up their eyes,
To drink in all the warmth.
Before the long day dies.

The dark blue sky
Lingering in the west,
Quickly fades away
To end its nightly quest.

Light in all its glory
Floods the eastern sky;
Filling all the heavens
With its joyous, glad cry.

A new day is born,
And new life to live;
A gift to all the world;
The best that God could give.

DOMESTIC VIOLENCE

Yvonne L. Hoffman

Editor's note: This is a paper written for a college course. It originally contained pinpoint cites to the works quoted. In the interest of readability these pinpoint cites have been removed. If desired, these citations can be obtained from the author or publisher.

In recent years the issue of domestic violence has extended to affect every economic and social stratum of society. Domestic violence is violence which occurs in the family unit. The definition of battery as presented in *Black's Law Dictionary,* written by Henry Campbell, MA, is as follows: "Any unlawful beating, or other wrongful physical violence or constraint, inflicted on a human being without his consent" (Goodrum v. State, 60 Ga. 511). According to the article "Violence at Home: When a Woman Needs a Way Out," printed in the June 1990 issue of *The Good Housekeeping Magazine,* "More than four million women are the victims of domestic violence each year." It also states that "A woman is battered every 15 seconds in the United States and 95% of batterers are men. In about half of these cases, children are also battered." The prevalence of domestic violence in the United States demands a greater public awareness of the problem, changes in the psychological behavior of both perpetuators and their victims, and changes in existing laws to protect women and children from abuse.

The author and psychologist Lenore E. Walker states in her book, *Terrifying Love: Why Women Kill and How Society Responds,* that public opinion often blames the victim and avoids involvement in incidents of domestic violence as it considers the abuse to be a family problem. She states further that the level of public awareness and its attitude toward domestic violence must be raised so that it may more effectively support the laws against family abuse. And that only through the educational system, use of the media, and changes in the law, will public opinion focus its attention on the issue of domestic violence.

Psychiatric attitudes must also change before positive effects can be made on the treatment of battered women. In her book *Stopping Wife Abuse: A Guide to the Emotional, Psychological and Legal Implications For the Abused Woman and Those Helping Her,* Jennifer Baker Fleming writes: "Members of the judiciary, law-enforcement personnel, medical doctors, and others with whom the abuse victim is likely to come in contact, all tend to adopt the explanation for behavior put forth by the psychiatric establishment." She says that throughout history, to the days of Sigmund Freud, women have been subordinated to men. The author also states that Freudism holds that "male violence against women . . . is not perceived as a problem, but as the natural masculine, aggressive response to women's innate masochism." This theory is not based on fact and until this is understood, negative attitudes on this subject will prevail.

In the writer Walker's opinion, the psychological behavior of both perpetuators and their victims of domestic violence results in a cycle of abuse and suffering. This cycle, caused by physical, emotional, and psychological dependence of the victim on her abuser, is defined as "learned helplessness" by psychologists. It is called "The Battered Women's Syndrome." The three phases of the cycle consist of the tension building phase, the acute battering incident, and the non-violent phase. Just recently the Battered Women's Syndrome has been admitted into the courts as evidence in defense of victims of abuse.

Studies show that the roles which men and women play in their relationships often end in violence. Men sometimes consider women as "possessions:" less than human. They use physical violence to control and dominate women. Many women accept the role of the subdominant partner and they practice appeasement to avoid abuse. This behavior on the part of both men and women can lead to spousal rape and murder of women by men, and of men by women in self-defense. Author Ann Marie Boylan, in her book *Adult Domestic Violence: Constitutional, Legislative, and Equitable Issues* states: "Referring generally to the frequency of rape within an ongoing intimate relationship, almost a third of 174 rape victims seen in a hospital emergency room over a two year period had histories as battered women."

Most authorities on the subject of domestic violence agree that only when the behavior of both perpetuators and their victims change will the incidence of domestic violence lessen. They assert that women must realize their value as persons, avoid negative roles thrust upon them by society, and learn to communicate their true feelings to their partners. They also advise women not to allow themselves to be "brainwashed" by men and know that they are not helpless. Finally, it is suggested that women should not accept verbal or physical abuse and they must seek professional aid before a tragedy occurs. Martin Blinder, MD, in his book *Lovers, Killers, Husbands, and Wives* advises: "To disassociate oneself from the reality of being abused does not eliminate the violence; instead, it contributes to its continuance." Blinder claims that women want to believe that their abusers are "sorry" and that "he will never do it again." He warns that women must realize that there is no reconciling the unreconcilable. He also advises that "Men must realize that marriage is a partnership between equal partners and not look upon women as 'possessions'." They should not use verbal or physical abuse to obtain control and dominance of women. Batterers must seek professional help to try to understand their behavior and enter a rehabilitation program.

New laws and changes in existing laws to protect abused women and children must be sought. Walker addresses this problem by stating, "Family law has been found to be riddled with both overt and subtle gender bias by commissioned state task forces studying the problem." Author and reporter John Leo, in the October 8, 1990 issue of the *U.S. News & World Report,* in his article "Rape is Not an Act of Bias," writes that The Violence Against Women Act of 1990 provides stronger penalties for repeat rape offenders, allowing their victims to sue them in federal court. It also makes judicial protective orders for women applicable across state lines. The bill is written in a gender-biased wording, but it is a law which will put strength in the enforcement of the capture and punishment of the offenders of this crime.

It is generally agreed upon by all parties concerned with the problem of domestic violence, that changes in the attitudes of the law and of the courts must be made before progress in the protection of battered women can proceed. Prevailing attitudes of the law are clearly shown in a statement written by Boylan: "An Arkansas feminist who has been working with abuse victims in a rural county suggested that the law was not intended as a serious attack on wife abuse but as something with which to counter feminist complaints about failure to ratify the Equal Rights Amendment. She feels that in rural areas, the law has not led to greater consciousness or effectiveness . . . ."

A recent change in the law is due to the introduction of The Battered Women's Syndrome by Lenore E. Walker, professor of psychology at the University of Denver. She writes that it may now be presented as evidence in the courts in cases of abuse by the defendants. Though the presiding judge of a California case in 1988 limited the testimony admitted, the jury heard about The Battered Women's Syndrome. They still found the defendant guilty of second-degree murder, instead of deliberating that she had acted in self-defense against her husband. The limitations imposed by the judge resulted in another woman being further abused by the court system. She says that the law is clear about justifiable homicide. "If a person holds a reasonable belief that she or he needs to defend her or himself from imminent death or bodily injury, then the homicide can be found to be justified. That is called self-defense." Jan Berliner Statman, in her book *The Battered Women's Survival Guide: Breaking the Cycle* insists that sources of aid for the victims of abuse must be provided by the authorities and they must give information about these sources to the public. Some sources available are: the Church, a counselor, a psychologist, a hospital, the police, or a Battered Women's Shelter. An alternative to the police is the "National Hotline" a service of the National Coalition Against Violence (1-800-333 SAFE or 1-800-333-7233).

The article "Violence at Home: When a Woman Needs a Way Out," provides some good advice for those battered women who must find a way out of their situation. It suggests that the first thing a battered woman must do is to get away. She must not be led to believe that the abuse will stop because the same patterns of violence exist and the battering will begin again. She must keep some cash, credit cards, prescriptions, checkbook, and set of house and car keys in a safe place. She should secure photocopies of the following: marriage license, driver's license, photo ID, birth certificates, Social Security cards, and all pertinent legal papers.

The article also stresses that battered women must report a battering immediately and ask to receive a police report and photos taken of her injuries. She can legally protect herself from her abuser by filing in court for a protective or restraining order. It will require the accused batterer to stay away. She can also file for a *temporary* custody of the children at the same time. If she cannot afford a lawyer, she may qualify for help from a legal services program, a court, or a domestic-violence advocate, who can help her to file the petitions.

In my opinion, the consequences of domestic violence are devastating; not only does its victim lose her self-esteem and makes her dependent on her abuser, but it often leaves her with no home or financial support. She must face the courts for redress where she is discriminated against by existing laws and gender bias. It leaves the abuser, with his pattern of violence, to work his havoc on the victim again. It also destroys the family unit. The children are often abused also, which leaves them with physical and traumatic injury. The example of violence occurring in the home is likely to be repeated by the children when they become adults.

As a foster parent for many years, I worked many times with children from homes broken by domestic violence. Some of the children had been abused or were present when their mothers were abused. They were abused in a way that affected every facet of their lives. They performed poorly in school and caused disturbances in the classroom. Most had difficulty in making friends and getting along with their teachers. At home, these children also had difficulty in relating to their new foster family because they could not trust anyone. Many of the children reacted violently to every situation.

Domestic violence strikes at the very heart of human relationships. It destroys trust between those who claim to love one another. When this love is replaced with hate and anger, it leaves its victims with damaged psyches and the permanent scars of trauma. Only through changes in the attitudes of the public, the law and its courts, and the psychological behavior of both the abusers and the abused will domestic violence be eliminated.

WORKS CITED

Black, Henery Campbell, M.A. *Black's Law Dictionary.* West
Publishing Co. St. Paul, Minn. 1968. (Goodrum v. State, 60 Ga.
511).

Blinder, Martin, M.D. *Lovers, Killers, Husbands and Wives.*
(N.P.)

Boylan, Ann Marie & Taub, Nadine. *Adult Domestic Violence:
Constitutional, Leqislative, and Equitable Issues.* (Tenn. Code Ann.
39-105. 180). Legal Services Corp., Research Institute, Wash. D.C.
1981).

Fleming, Jennifer Baker. *Stoppinq Wife Abuse: A Guide to the
Emotional, Psycholoqical, and Leqal Implications For the Abused
Woman and Those Helping Her.* Anchor Books, Anchor
Press/Doubleday. Garden City, N.Y.

Leo, John. "Rape is Not an Act of Bias." *U.S. News & World
Report Magazine.* U.S. News & World Report, Inc. Wash. D.C.
Oct.8, 1990.

Statman, Jan Berliner. *The Battered Women's Survival Guide:
Breakinq the Cycle.* Dallas, Texas. Taylor. 1990.

"Violence at Home: When a Woman Needs a Way out." *The
Good Housekeeping Magazine.* June 1990.

Walker, Lenore E. *Terrifying Love: Why Women Kill and How
Society Responds.* Harper & Row. N.Y. 1989.

child, child

by Vickie L. Cook

child, child run and play
learn to put your hurts away
learn to run and jump and shout. . .
but never let your feelings out.

child, child dry those tears
put them away for years and years.
call it sunshine when it's rain
say it's laughter when it's pain.

child, child go and hide
put those big fears deep inside.
place them high upon a shelf
and hide them even from yourself.

child, child toss a stone
know that you are all alone. . .

child, child skip a rope
count to ten and give up hope.

PETS OR PROBLEMS

by Edith Erickson

It was a cool sunny spring morning. Papa harnessed the team, hitched them to the smaller wagon and was ready to go to the nearest little town, twelve miles away, where he would get supplies both for the house and for Mother's tiny store, which carried candy, gum, pencils, and tablets and maybe a few other articles.

Little Jimmy begged to go. The trip would take most of the day but Papa put an extra blanket in and let Jimmy go with him. It was always exciting to see what Papa came home from town with. Once in a long time there might even be a toy.

It was evening before the travelers got home. The children rushed to see what was in the wagon. Surprise! In a box near the high wagon seat there were two bummer lambs.

On the way home Papa had stopped to let the horses rest near where a band of sheep were feeding in a nearby field. The herder came over to the wagon to talk a bit. As he looked at little Jimmy he said, "Don't you want a bummer? I have a couple I need to get rid of."

A bummer is a lamb that the mother will have nothing to do with. It must be bottle fed. If a person has more that a handful of sheep there is no time to fool with an abandoned lamb.

Papa had never had sheep on the ranch so he thought raising a lamb would be a good experience for the children and when fall came, mutton for the harvesters would be a nice change. He gave the herder fifty cents. Put some supplies on the wagon floor so that the lambs could be put into a box.

The lambs were ready to be fed as soon as they were taken out of the wagon. The children giggled as they watched the little tails wiggle as Papa fed them warmed cow's milk.

The first few times everyone wanted to hold the bottle so they could try to touch the fast moving tail and feel their soft wool. Mother soon heard things as, "It's my turn." "No, it isn't you did it last time." "That one is mine, don't touch it." "No, it's mine."

It was not long before the dialogue changed to, "It's your turn. I did it last night."

Mother soon put up a chart to see that everyone did their share because she had to do it while the children were at school and she wasn't about to be stuck with it in the evening.

To make it easy for her to take care of them a little pen was built in the woodshed which was close to the house. On sunny days they were turned out on the lawn where like all young animals they could romp and play as well as begin to nibble the green grass, but milk was still their main food.

A person can't just say "Lamb or Sheep" when talking to or about an animal. They soon became Susie and Sally. Now Susie was more aggressive and inquisitive with Sally perfectly happy to follow behind. Susie was soon racing up the back porch steps as soon as the kitchen door was opened. She knew that was where the food came from. It took Sally a bit longer to master the stairs. As they got a little larger they discovered it was great fun to bounce stiff legged around the porch that extended nearly all the way around the house. What fun to make that echoing sound from a wooden porch.

Soon they were darting into the house. The first door that they tried was the kitchen. They knew that was where the food came from. They soon learned that they were not welcome in that door. Mother used the broom on them whenever they popped into her work area. Next they tried the front door, which led into a big front hall. In that big hall Mother had a country post office and a little store so many people came and went, especially at mail time and after school. The little rascals would watch until there was a lot of activity, then suddenly dash in among the people and hide under or behind the counter, among the packages or under or behind whatever struck their fancy. Many people laughed and thought that they were cute.

Mother would not put up with this for very long. Soon she stated firmly that they must be moved from the yard. By that time they did not need to be fed so often. They were taken to the barn lot and it was expected that they would stay there, but no such luck. The barn yard and the lawn were separated by a rock wall along the front of the lawn and a set of stairs coming up to the end of the sidewalk. The stairs had always prevented animals from entering the yard. This was not true with these two sheep. The stairs were no challenge to them. As soon as the barn door was open the lambs came on the run from the barn, up the front steps, across the lawn, up the porch steps, and into the front hall as soon as someone opened the door.

This time they were banished to the feed lot west of the house. Surely this would be a comfortable place where they would be content to stay. No one thought about the stile that went over the back fence. In no time at all the curious lambs had investigated the ten acre pasture and again found steps they could climb.

Across the back yard they came. Up the kitchen steps, bounce, bounce, bounce, around the porch to the front door and in they came. They were captured, put back into the pasture and the stile was removed.

Before harvest time everyone knew that no one could possibly eat mutton that fall. It was decided that the two sheep would be the beginning of a larger flock.

When the snow fell and weather became cold the sheep were moved to the calf barn where they were more protected. One morning after a heavy snowfall, they discovered a way to get out into the barn yard. Papa was sweeping the front porch and steps. When the now full grown sheep saw him near their favorite door they came on the run, up two sets of steps and pushed on the door. Papa had not closed it tight enough that it latched so the push made it fly open. They discovered something that they had never really noticed before. There were no people in the hall, but there was a flight of stairs longer than any that they had ever climbed. Those led to the second story of the house. Up they went, bounce, bounce, bounce, down the long hardwood hall to where Mother was just finishing dressing. She shook her apron at them, hustling them back down the hall, the long stairs, out the front door and off the porch. With one final flip of her apron a terrible thing happened. When Mother got up in the morning she always put her lower dental plate in her apron pocket until she had time to brush her teeth and get ready for the day. Those teeth flew out of her pocket and into the soft fluffy snow. Off and on all day and for several days, the family hunted for the lost teeth but to no avail. There were too many tracks and the teeth could not be found.

The sheep were banished to the pig barn where a section was remodeled for them. There they spent the next few months until both of them had twin lambs in the spring and once again roamed the green pasture.

This was the beginning of a good sized band of sheep. Each spring they had two or sometimes even three lambs. If that third lamb became a bummer it was never, never raised in the yard or anywhere near the house. Both of the original "bummers" lived to be a ripe old age but never forgot how to climb steps and were always considered pets and not just two old ewes. If a gate happened to be left open they always had to check out that special front door that had such interesting steps.

For their whole lives they continued to be pets and also problems.

RIGGS CEMETERY

by Dick Warwick

All day the granite stone
steeped in sunlight, molecules
vibrating, humming, energy
quickening above the grave
of a man dead seventy years.
The dry topsoil grows weeds—
downy brome—"cheat grass"—
but nobody cheats death here, this
is death's domain, this windy hilltop
with a forever view.

The land undulates, a wave
at the top of its crest
holds this dead community
of several dozen souls.
Most born before the land was
broken and planted,
some from the "old country"—
they come together
held in earthy suspension
in this sea of loess. A warm gravestone
holds the heat of the sun gone down.
And it holds the name of a person,
though lichen nibbles at the symbols
and no one has thought to place flowers here
perhaps for decades.

This hilltop was never cultivated.
It is a haven for lilacs run riot,
a few trees scrawny from thirst,
and weeds, refugees from cropland.
It has seen, no doubt,
more trysts than funerals;

more beer busts than wakes,
more picnics than vigil fasts. It is
after all, a place for the living.
I feel wraithlike, insubstantial
as smoke, moving among
these lithic, silent forms;
who have stood unmoved while a century
of melodrama wailed and giggled,
cried and raged around them;
who hold their inscripted names
like bouquets of dry
and scentless blossoms.
Here remembrance, like letters incised
on an alabaster obelisk,
has melted; memories move on
with these dusty dunes, old names
sound quaint, and call to mind
no face.

This graveyard—
it is not actually a door
into another world, as we often suppose.
It is a dump, a midden,
and more here lies forgotten
than will ever be recalled.
There is no grail here
to be dug from the soil, shining.
But it is high and peaceful, and it does
catch the first and last light
as the sun is born, and dies.

These monuments are the only rock
in this land of fine soil.
They are out of place here, milestones
for marking time.
But as twilight deepens, their warmth
is a comfort, and every stone-marked grave
radiates the gone sun's heat.

I visit Riggs Cemetery now and then
to lean against these warm forms
and to enjoy the view;
to visit these voiceless, unreferenced names,
to look once more
out toward the darkening horizon.
Today was—June 9, 1994.

A HOMECOMING

by J. Kay Krom

I was just seven years old in 1943 when we learned my adored older brother, Robert A. Baker, was coming home on furlough after serving in the United States Army. Bob had been sent to Europe where he was wounded and had spent some time in a military hospital recuperating prior to this scheduled homecoming.

The war years remain a vivid memory from my impressionable youth. Our entire family listened intently to radio broadcasts for news from the front, and every word in the newspapers was eagerly devoured in order to keep abreast of the latest news of the war effort.

A popular song of the time was titled *My Buddy* but our family personalized the lyrics, and we felt it was our very own song about my brother. I recall my mother playing that record on the Philco phonograph and I sang along, "Our Bobby, Our Bobby. . ."

During those war years we lived in Spokane, the hub of the Inland Empire. My mother had a rather large extended family and I treasure the many old black and white photographs of all the handsome young cousins and uncles posing in their various uniforms as they stood on our modest front porch while passing through the city.

Like all families at the time we were involved in the war effort. My dad was a night guard at the aluminum mills in Trentwood and he raised a prolific victory garden that provided fruits and vegetables which mother canned insuring delicious winter-time meals. She also worked at the neighborhood grocery store, and we all saved tin, rubber, aluminum, or anything else deemed reusable for the war. Our blue service star hung proudly from the front window, and we made every effort to buy war bonds as our tight budget would allow, and the family used our food and gas stamps prudently.

At last we were notified that Bob was coming home and would be arriving by train. We were to meet him at the bustling Railroad Depot which is now the Amtrak Station. We were up bright and early and we crammed into the family coupé for the drive to the station in eager anticipation of this long-awaited day.

The building looked enormous to a child, and even at the early hour it was teeming with people. My dad, mom, older sister, Bob's young wife and myself were there, bursting with excitement, pride and relief. We learned the train would be delayed causing a nerve-racking wait. All morning my folks had repeatedly admonished me to hold back and let Bob's wife be the first to greet him and then it would be my turn. At long last we heard the conductor's voice announcing the arrival of his train! I was so excited I could scarcely breathe. Service men and women of all description were departing, and the crowd seemed crushing. We scanned each passing face and suddenly he appeared, looking so strong and handsome, grinning broadly. By this time I had reached the bursting point and had managed to completely forget the repeated admonishment. I ran as swiftly as I could while dodging the throng of people. Our eyes locked, he dropped his bags and caught me in mid-air as I jumped in his arms with my skinny little legs around his waist, arms around his neck. The rest of the family gathered around, forming our own tight little circle. For a moment we were all speechless, caught up in our intense emotions, tears freely flowing. Looking back at the scene, I later realized it was the only time I saw my stoic father actually cry.

It remains a moment that years seem unable to dim, one of those magical moments filled with pure love and indescribable joy.

HOME OPENER

by Jeff Lageson

That most perverse of American pastimes,
where tens of thousands pay hard earned money
to watch arrogant young millionaires play
tag and catch,
women ogle tight male buns,
a cup of cheap beer costs four bucks,
men say they could do that
and kids just know they'll be there someday.
God, I love baseball.

THE ELEVATOR

by Steve Kenworthy

Jim Foreman was thinking about the Johnson account as he drove to work on the freeway that morning. The account was an example of "Murphy's Law" in its purest form. Anything and everything that could go wrong had reared up to slap Jim and all his hard work in the face. Now, after almost eight months, there were just a few more wrinkles to be worked out. He began thinking of the well-deserved vacation he would take as soon as everything had been taken care of. It had been almost two years since his last vacation, and he desperately felt the need to get away with Margaret and the kids. His marriage had been teetering on the rocks since the first problems with the Johnson account.

The traffic seemed to be moving much slower than usual and Jim was beginning to get irritated. He knew just exactly how traffic jams got started. . . by two idiots. The first idiot would try to enter the freeway at twenty-five miles per hour, and the second idiot would slow down to let him on. From there things always deteriorated to gridlock.

It was less than a mile to Jim's exit, but Jim knew that it would be almost an hour before he reached his destination. He left reality again to think about his upcoming vacation. Daydreaming had the wonderful effect of transporting him through time so that soon he was searching for a parking space in the basement garage of his firm's high-rise office building.

Jim worked on the twenty-eighth floor, right between personnel on the twenty-seventh and accounting on the twenty-ninth. He liked the view from his office and was thinking of that view when he boarded the elevator in the parking garage. There was no one in the elevator as he climbed aboard. The canned music was playing a song that he liked, so he decided to ride all the way to the executive offices on the fortieth floor to talk with his boss, Bill Dikeman, about the Johnson account.

As Jim stepped off the elevator on the fortieth floor he noticed Bill Dikeman's secretary coming out of Bill's office. She carefully and quietly closed the door behind her, which almost certainly meant that Bill Dikeman was in an important meeting. Jim debated whether or not to stop and chat with the secretary. He decided in the interest of all concerned that it wasn't necessary.

Jim turned quickly in hopes of catching the elevator but was too late, as someone had called it up to the top floor. Jim thought that unusual. The thought soon left him as he concentrated more on his work for the day.

Jim pressed the 'down' button and began waiting. The thought occurred to him that the other elevator may be quicker. He abandoned the idea of checking it out when he saw the lights above the elevator indicate that it had already begun its descent.

When the elevator arrived and the doors opened, Jim noticed there were two men in the elevator, neither of whom Jim knew nor recognized. That seemed odd, for he thought he knew all the executives from the thirty-eighth floor and above since, in one way or another, they were all his superiors. Jim nodded a greeting as he entered the elevator. The two men seemed not to notice and Jim really didn't care. He was not a socially-minded person, especially when it came to meeting new people.

Jim pushed the button to the twenty-eighth floor and moved to the back of the elevator. He watched the indicator lights move slowly from floor to floor and drifted off in thought again. Jim didn't notice until the lights indicated the eighteenth floor that he had missed his floor. As he reflected on it he realized that he had not missed his floor, but that the elevator had not stopped at his floor to let him off. He went to the panel of buttons and pushed the button for the twenty-eighth floor several times, knowing logically that this was futile since the elevator was descending and the twenty-eighth floor was now above him. To his surprise and contempt, the elevator continued its descent.

"Damn elevator!" The words escaped in his frustration. Jim disliked profanity and was embarrassed that he had used the expression around these men whom he assumed must be either colleagues or superiors. The two men seemed not to notice Jim or his dilemma.

"Excuse me, but could one of you try the buttons on your panel?" Jim asked the two men, wondering if it was just the panel on his side of the car that was inoperative. The two men ignored him.

"Excuse me. . ." Jim said again, to no avail. He was getting fed up with the whole situation and decided it was time for some affirmative action. He pressed the emergency stop button. Nothing happened. Rather than embarrass himself again by speaking, Jim maneuvered to the other side of the elevator and went through his button-pushing tactics on the second panel. Again there was no response from the elevator or the two men.

Jim looked up at the indicator lights. He noticed that they were not traveling faster than normal and dismissed the fears he had about broken cables and such. He decided that it must be a simple malfunction.

At last he felt the slowing of the car and noticed that the lights indicated they were stopping at the lobby. Jim glanced at the panel and noticed for the first time that the light indicating the lobby level was the only one that had lit. He was going to complain to maintenance as soon as he got off. He knew it was probably no one's fault, but to complain to someone would at least make him feel better. He wondered at the same time if he should mention the rude strangers on the elevator to someone. He was nearly as angry at them as he was at the elevator.

As the doors opened to the lobby, Jim noticed that the two men were going to exit and waited for them. That was a mistake. People late for work began filing in. Jim made a weak effort to warn them about the elevator's recently acquired taste for belligerency. The passengers didn't seem to care.

Jim's concerns turned to leaving the crowded elevator. Just as he reached the door it closed. He thrust his arm through, knowing that the doors would re-open fro him. They didn't. Jim felt the grip of the doors grow tighter and felt fortunate that he was able to pull his arm in at all. He looked around and saw twenty or so people who didn't seem to notice him. He made a comment to one of them about his arm and the doors. The man ignored Jim, remaining in his own private world.

Jim began to think the whole world had gone mad. He tried to count to ten slowly, in order to regain his composure. He forced himself through the crowd to where he could again confront one of the operating panels. He pushed the button for the twenty-eighth floor again. After all, the elevator had taken him up to the fortieth floor earlier without any problems. It may be that descending was the elevator's only problem. Jim had almost convinced himself. He began to relax.

He couldn't help feeling a bit strange. There were at least twenty or so people who entered the lift at the lobby. Jim didn't recognize any of them. This made him uncomfortable, but there was something else still—all these people had the same expression on their faces. There were none that were happy; none that were sad; none that were anxious, agitated, calm or scared. In fact, the weird thing about them was the complete lack of expression. Then a frightening thought struck him. All the people on the elevator had the same face as the two men who had ridden down the elevator with Jim. The same eyes, nose mouth—everything was the same, as if they were clones of the first pair. Jim was horrified. Frantically he began pushing buttons. There was no reaction—not from the elevator, not from the other passengers.

Jim began to sweat. His mind was racing as he thought of all the possible explanations—a game? a trick? an illusion? He looked up at the indicator lights and was semi-mesmerized by their incessant methodical ascension. Jim pinched himself and immediately felt silly. He had checked to see if he was dreaming. Then he felt the sweat on his brow and became self-conscious. He looked around to see if anyone was staring. Of course, they weren't.

Jim made a super-human effort to regain control of his thoughts. He noticed that the elevator was approaching the twenty-eighth floor. He convinced himself that the elevator was going to stop and soon he would be seated at his desk.

The elevator passed the twenty-sixth floor. It reached the twenty-seventh floor. Jim was sure he felt the elevator slow a bit. The twenty-eighth floor—home—security—sanity. Just as Jim began to move toward the door he realized the elevator had not stopped. Panic struck his heart and he felt as if he were going to die. Jim felt himself screaming, but heard nothing. He fought his way back to the panel and beat upon the buttons. He pushed the emergency stop until his fingers ached. He could not believe this was happening. The elevator continued its climb. Jim closed his eyes and prayed. He prayed because he knew that no one on earth could hear him.

Before he opened his eyes Jim sensed the slowing of the elevator. Yes, he was positive that the elevator was coming to a stop. He felt the jerk as it came to rest. Maybe there was a God after all.

The doors slid open and Jim spilled from the car in a flood of relief. He was so glad to be free that at first he didn't notice that the elevator had deposited him on the roof. His reaction upon noticing his whereabouts was one of surprise. He had no idea that the elevator went to the roof. Then the next thought was even more sobering—if he had a choice of the roof or the lobby he would much prefer the lobby, even if it meant returning to his moving prison. He spun around to climb aboard an elevator for the last time in his life, but the expressionless passengers prevented re-entry. They continued to pour from the elevator as if it were a great hall filled with people. Jim knew that there had been only twenty or so people in the elevator. Now there were throngs coming from the open jaws that had already devoured Jim's soul. Trying with all his might, he was still unable to overcome the flood of nothings that assaulted him. Finally the doors closed and the elevator began its trek downward. Jim stood isolated in a great crowd. From where he was standing he could see the elevator shaft, but it was as inaccessible to him as if it were a thousand miles away. Jim was losing his mind.

The view was beautiful. Even better than the view from Jim's office. Jim sat on a small vent and, as calmly as he could, surveyed the situation. It appeared that there were now two or three hundred people on the roof. Every few minutes the elevator would arrive and disgorge its hoards of expressionless faces. All were ignoring their situation, each other, and Jim. Each time the elevator would arrive, Jim futility tried to fight his way through the ever-increasing crowd. The elevator delivered more casualties with each trip. Jim shouted warning to their deaf ears without success.

New panic crept into Jim's soul. He noticed that he was on the outer circle of people. As each group arrived he was forced further from the elevator and closer to the edge. In a sudden expression of horror he stretched as high as he could on his toes to survey the crowd. The roof was now very crowded. The edge was only a few feet away. Another group arrived and Jim was pushed even nearer the edge. He fought hard to break through the crowd. He had to cushion himself from the abyss. It was no use. The crowd had grown so thick it was impenetrable.

Jim cried. He thought of Margaret, his kids, and the vacation he would never take. He thought of the Johnson account. He thought of Bill Dikeman in his important meeting on the fortieth floor. He thought of death.

Jim was at the edge now. One more group from the elevator and there would be no more room. In the distance he could see the indicator lights on the elevator. It was almost to the roof. Jim saw it arrive. He saw the doors open. He closed his eyes and saw nothing else.

***

The police car had effectively blocked off traffic. A sergeant and a detective were bent over a bloody limp shape.

"Did anyone see him jump?" asked the detective.

"One man here on the street saw the whole thing," replied the sergeant. "He said that this guy stood on the edge for a minute and then just fell."

"No one else was up there?"

"No one."

DAMNED BLACK HOLE

by Vickie L. Cook

I wasn't looking where I walked and slipped into
that damn black hole
f
  a
   l
    l
     i
      n
       g
again.
Like Death without dying. Like midnight without the hope of
dawn.
"Hey up there, would someone toss me down a Prozac."

RED FLAG AGAINST
WHITE SNOW

Susan J. Hallett

"Sometime when you're out in Edwards Mill, stop by to see Emma Brazelton. She might like to use our van for getting to the doctor occasionally. Last time I ran into her, she said that she didn't drive anymore in the winter." The agency transportation director was putting a bug in my ear again. She was good at doing that and she was usually right.

And so I found myself sitting in Emma's living room on an early spring day when crocus and lingering frost both clung to the shaded flower bed by the apartment house door. She was in her seventies, a large-boned woman with a surprising amount of gray hair heaped on her head and warm-hearted brown eyes. She had all but forced coffee on me, not knowing that I disliked it but was learning to drink my share on home visits, generously mellowed with milk and sugar.

I explained that I often stopped in to see retired people and inform them of the various services offered by my agency, such as transportation and home-delivered meals. She listened with appropriate interest and I sensed she was trying to help me do my job well. She didn't drive during the winter and had difficulty recently getting to a medical appointment in the city some ninety miles away. She took the proffered brochure on our van program and set it inside her phone book for future reference.

I looked around the room and noticed several oil paintings on the nearby walls.

"Does someone you know like to paint?"

"Those are mine," she said. I got up to look more closely. Scenes of rural life, a white wooden farmhouse with a large black dog in the yard, a country lane bordered by wildflowers, a farm kitchen with wood stove and rag rug.

"I write the name of one of my grandkids on the back of each one as I finish it," she said.

"That will give each of them something very special from their grandmother someday," said I. "How long have you been painting?"

She told me that when she was a child, her family lived on a small dirt farm trying to make ends meet. She made it sound as though they produced dirt and I suddenly had a sense of poverty and childish yearning. There had been a paint set in the Sears catalog, but never a possibility of obtaining it.

Then had come marriage, children, another dirt farm, this time on the Palouse, and with the war, gradually improving finances. Her husband had passed away a couple of years ago. After his death, she said to herself, "Well, if I don't do it now, when will I?" So she bought art supplies, took a few lessons, and began recording the world for her grandchildren to see through her eyes.

I noticed one painting hung near her chair, small but compelling. It looked as though she was working with perspective, for a mailbox with red flag raised stood on a post in the middle of a snowy winter scene. The mailbox, and especially the flag, seemed almost surreal.

"That was my first painting," she said. And she told me the story behind it. She and her husband William used to live in a fifty year old farmhouse some two miles up a private lane from the graveled county road. It was there they raised their four children along with grain and a few head of cattle. After retirement they leased out the farmland and continued to enjoy their country home. The kids, themselves living on the west side of the state and beyond, had suggested that they move to town, but Emma and William weren't ready yet.

Winter bothered the kids most. Some years it didn't snow enough for the county road crew to bother plowing the gravel road, while in others their lane drifted shut until the tenant got around to plowing them out. A few days of being snowbound didn't bother them, what with a well-stocked pantry and the comfort of the wood stove in the kitchen. Emma, William and their black lab Gabe rather enjoyed settling on the oval rag rug near the stove with the cold wind and snow blowing past the sink window.

Three winters ago, though, a combination of events transformed their comfortable refuge into a frightening place. William always got up a little earlier than Emma to build the fire and start the coffee. She fell back to sleep one morning after he left the bed and awoke with a start some time later. The house was quiet, absent the sound of crackling wood and the scent of freshly brewing coffee. She hurried downstairs to the kitchen to find William lying on the kitchen floor. He was unconscious and saliva drooled from the comer of his mouth. She checked to be sure that he was breathing and brought pillow and blanket to make him more comfortable. Then she hurried to phone the volunteer ambulance.

It was early November and the phone was out. That happened occasionally, they usually blamed it on the weather or "hunters" and service was always restored within a day. But a day seemed a terribly long time to wait that morning. To make things worse, this was shaping up to be one of the snowy winters and the wind had been tearing at the house all night before settling into an exhausted calm before dawn. Several inches of snow had blown wildly around house and yard and she knew without looking that the lane had drifted shut. Their tenant had gone elk hunting down in the Blue Mountains that week and was due to return on Sunday. In this weather he would be lucky to get home himself. No one would be pushing a plow down that road anytime soon.

She found herself becoming frantic. She knelt down and shook William by the shoulder. He did not respond and was too heavy to move. Gabe nudged her anxiously, and looking into the dog's worried eyes, she got an idea. She rearranged pillow and blanket once more and left the room.

A few moments later she reappeared bundled up and sweating in the warm kitchen. At least the furnace was working. She grabbed the kitchen broom and called to Gabe to join her. He galloped across the kitchen floor and burst out the back door into the snowy yard. After capering around for a moment, the lab joined her in walking up the lane to the county road.

Cold temperatures had produced snow like sifted white flour, more like walking through the volcanic ash blown in from Mount St. Helens than the wetter, heavier snow winter usually brought. Mercifully the wind had stopped although she knew at any moment it could transform sky and landscape into a single universe of blowing white. She found herself remembering stories that her old granny had told her of travelers lost in snowstorms, bodies not recovered until the spring thaw. She thought of William lying on the kitchen floor. Using the broom as a walking stick, she marched determinedly along.

In pleasant weather she and William looked forward to their daily walk out to the mailbox on the county road. It took them an hour or so, though in bad weather they used the car. The lab knew exactly where she was headed this morning and gamboled along looking for adventure. It was hard to walk through knee high drifts and she found herself tiring. The snow flew up at the slightest touch into little clouds.

She found herself thinking of the lane in June, when each bend produced its own blend of wild flowers. There were several different kinds of daisies, yellow and green. Blue and purple lupine spiked upward next to bachelor buttons in maroon, white, blue, purple, lavender and a dozen other colors. Her daughter Anne had studied wild flowers at college and knew the proper names for many of them. The daisies, for instance, weren't really daisies, but were composed of several species, such as arrowleaf balsam root. She couldn't keep all that straight, but loved how they waved in the breeze against the pale blue sky of early summer.

And the birds. Chinese pheasants sailing across their path, magpies comically arguing over an egg they had found, red-winged blackbirds near the culvert where winter runoff watered cattails. High overhead red-tailed hawks called to one another while traveling to a favored hunting spot and insects added a solid wall of sound to the rustle of miles and miles of young wheat, brushing softly against itself in the breeze. She focused her mind on June while walking through November.

After what seemed like hours she arrived at the intersection of the lane and the county road. The road crew had been by and plowed the snow into high banks on either side of the road. Apparently they were hoping the wind wouldn't resume blowing either. She looked down several feet from the top of the bank to the road and wondered what to do next.

After a moment she turned her back to the road, sank to her knees, and slid on her stomach all the way down, dragging the broom behind her. She landed hard on the road and lay there quietly for a moment. Then she got up and walked to her mailbox as if this were an ordinary morning. She pulled an envelope from her pocket, placed it in the mailbox, and raised the red flag to alert Lonnie, the mailman. With the road freshly plowed, he would likely pass by later in the morning, near noon. She looked at Gabe, busy running up and down the county road so quiet this day, and said, "I've done what I can."

Getting home was worse than walking out, at least getting back up that bank was. It took her a long time to climb up and a bone-chilling ache spread through her body. She walked slowly up the lane, thinking of the warm kitchen and William's need of her. At last she turned the final bend, where tangles of wild roses slept beneath the snow, and the house lay in front of her. The lab bounded to the door and looked at her with impatience, eager for a belated breakfast.

In the house William remained unchanged, his breathing slow and somewhat ragged, his pulse irregular. One side of his body was cold to the touch. She fed the dog, but did not eat herself, settling after a time in her rocker next to William on the rug, listening to the fire work its way through the wood.

That afternoon she jumped at the sound of engines approaching the house. Hurrying to the window she saw the county plow pushing into the yard, followed by the ambulance, followed by Lonnie in his four wheel drive. And the emotion she had controlled until then welled up and she began to sob.

William had suffered a stroke and did not recover well. He responded poorly during rehab and was eventually placed in the nursing home at Edwards Mill. Emma moved into an apartment to be near him. The apartment felt empty and the management didn't allow large black labs. Eventually she began to fill the space up with paintings, starting with the mailbox and its red flag.

As I left her home that day, I was almost surprised to see evidence of spring outdoors, rather than snow drifts and an elderly woman walking with a kitchen broom and a black lab. I encouraged Emma once again to give the agency a call when she needed to go to the doctor and thanked her for the visit and the coffee. She had even suggested the names of several other residents in the apartment building who might appreciate a visit from me. She looked at me one last time with her warm brown eyes and said, "I'm glad you enjoyed the coffee. I do what I can."

LOVE IN THE PALM
OF YOUR HAND

by Della Evans

The Indians had some beautiful thoughts
Long ago when they roamed this land
One, that I like to contemplate is—
You should hold love in the palm of your hand.

I like to think about that just a bit
Love is such an all-encompassing word
But to hold it out a such
all that is described as love is offered.

It really is a beautiful thought
No tight fist around it
Just giving with no attachment—
The thought is really quite exquisite.

Consider the love of parent for child,
It is nothing short of grand
But really so much more, if only
It's held in the palm of your hand.

The feelings of friend for friend
Can be so very deep
But a loving friendship given freely
Will be the one you cherish and keep.

This too, is probably especially true
If you think you have found
That special one as a life-long mate,
Love in an open palm will know no bound.

And finally, I've realized this is the love

Our Father freely offers each day
And I pray to be worthy of His love
In some small way.

I think those Indian brothers of mine
For that thought they gave to me
To hold love in the palm of your hand
Is what real love should be.

THE HERD

by Tamara Riggle Muggoch

He could hear the wheezing from his own chest as he watched his breath rolling off into the frosty air. Walking up the hill, his leather-bound feet barely made a sound as they slipped through the ankle deep mud. The storm had dropped enough rain last night to make tracking the beast almost impossible, but years of searching for sign had helped. The birds started to scold again, recovering from the crash of the rifle shot.

The thrill of the hunt was receding into the drudgery of dragging the animal back to the barn. It was a small beast, but its total weight would make the half mile haul take the rest of the day and most of the night. He couldn't even gut it out because of the ritual. Neither could he make camp at dark to wait until morning, the wind and night time temperatures forced a man to keep moving, and the ritual only allowed so much time after the creature died. It had taken all day to find it, but he gave up the hope for any rest as the cold quickly stiffened his prey.

***

She had quit her job in the town many years before. It was better that she stay home to help him work the magic. After all this time, the people still called them ranchers, though they no longer tried to raise anything without the words. Even with the book they hadn't raised anything for many years, and were depending on this season to survive.

The fire crackled as she stirred the coals, the kettle was almost hot enough to start supper. She had heard the rifle shot, and knew she would be eating alone. If he missed, which he never had, he would keep searching. If the beast fell, it would take time to drag it home. Either way, it was good to know he had seen one so soon and so close.

Her biscuits and beans went down quickly and she cleared the table. Moving a chair to the book shelf, she climbed up and retrieved the old book. It's cover was worn and the pages bent, but it was her one dearest possession. She set it on the table and got out her knives. Checking their sharpness, she sliced open her thumb. She studied the wound and saw how it bled; it was a clean cut with no ragged edges. The knives would do without sharpening tonight. She wrapped her thumb with her kerchief and wiped the blade on her skirt.

She banked the fire and pulled on her boots. Reaching into the back of the cupboard, she brought out her lantern and lit it with the candle from the table. When the lamp had started to glow steadily, she blew out the candle flame and put on her coat. With the book under her blouse and the lantern in her hand, she put her knives in her pocket and headed out into the night.

***

She was almost done with the preparations when the barn door slid open. She was startled from her work for a moment, but looked around and saw that it was him. The wind came through the open door and the lantern light flickered. She went back to her work without a word, and he closed the door. He said nothing, knowing that all must be done in quiet for now. Warming his hands at the lantern, he waited for her to finish and stand up.

"Good hunt?" she asked as she straightened her legs.

He nodded and said "An old cow."

"The song, then." She went to the straw bale where the book lay and turned a grimy page. After so many years, she didn't need the written words, but felt better having the book nearby. As she started the song, she closed her eyes. Low sounds rolled off of her tongue, making the ancient language she had never known. Her body swayed and he listened for the right phrase.

Hearing the sounds he waited for, he began chanting his own version of the song. He sang softly beside her for a few minutes, then went to the barn door. Outside, the wind burned his ears. He bent his head down and whispered the old words to the dead beast. He began dragging it back through the open door, and could feel the warmth of the lantern behind him. She continued to sing as the animal was laid out before her. Then he repeated the words he had whispered outside, and all became quiet.

He walked to the door and pulled it closed. The wind whistled through the cracks in the weathered wood and he leaned against the door frame to watch her. She had already turned a page and was kneeling down beside the creature. The lantern light played off of her features, and he could see her mouthing the words. Gnarled hands moved quickly and the yellow light glinted off the blades. With one knife in each hand, she made short work of the carving. As fast as it went, he could see her concentrating on the lines and shapes. She never faltered.

Soon, her hands came to rest. She rocked back on her heels and wiped her bloody fingers on her skirt. Turning around to look at him, she smiled and he moved forward. As he came towards her, she cleaned the blades on her sleeves and stood up.

While she stepped aside to warm herself at the lantern, he began his work. Using the broken blade of his pocket knife as a mallet, he slightly flattened each of the hundreds of pieces. The work was slow, but thorough. When he had gone through them all, he changed to a sharp blade. He picked up each of the fist sized chunks of meat and carefully cut a tiny "R" into it. It was still their registered brand, though there were few people left to check it. Finishing, he wiped his blades clean and put the pocket knife away. She turned a few more pages in her book and they looked at their work. He asked "Ready?" and they put on their coats.

With the barn door wide open and the lantern turned down, they filled their arms and pockets with all of the meat they could carry. There was much left, and it would take many trips.

It was lunch time before they finished spreading out the beast. As they went, they carefully counted how many pieces they left in the corral, and how many were placed in each pasture. The chunks had to be set several yards apart, and nowhere very steep. The last few tiny pieces were left in the barn, and the two gathered their tools.

She carried the book under her blouse and he picked up the knives. The lantern had gone out hours ago, but the early afternoon light brought some warmth through the dusty windows. Their hands and feet were numb from the work of the night and morning, but their tired bodies were warm with pride and hope. They walked hand in hand back to the house to get their lunch, and to wait.

***

As they lay on their straw mats next to the fire, neither could sleep. The storm had blown over that afternoon, and the evening was clear and cold. Without the sound of the blowing wind, they could hear an owl hooting, and the howl of a lone wolf. He held her and they listened, and hoped. Day-break found them still exhausted, but sleeping fitfully. They awoke at the same time and realized that it was already late morning, a full day since they had finished their work. She looked at him with fear in her eyes, and he could feel her worry. They dressed quickly and rushed outside without their morning coffee.

The sun was high and the mud on the steps was starting to dry out. They started to run towards the corrals, but she slipped on the mud. He turned back to help her but she waved him away. "I'm okay. Go look."

She gathered her skirts around her knees and stepped past the puddles. He looked at her with concern but turned around and ran ahead.

As he crested the hill between the house and the pastures, the sun reflected off of the barn roof and blinded him. He stopped short and blinked hard.

He was still standing there, blinking and trying to catch his breath, when she came up behind him. He let out a huge yell and spun around to face her. He grinned and laughed, and then she saw.

The empty valley pastures where they had worked so long the day before were changed. Their footprints through the mud were smeared. The small chunks of animal flesh and their dark blood stains were completely gone; the hundreds of pieces had been transformed while the couple slept. They would survive, the herd was back.

SURGERY

by Jeff Lageson

A surreal day
like on TV
      the ceiling going by
      the doors opening
cold air
then, they tricked me with the gas
and I woke up with my wife
talking about my dog
feeling really, really sick
and feeling as though something happened
and someone important was there
yet I have no real memory
only a gap of time and a scar

WELCOME TO THE FARM

by Alisa M. Largent

Several years ago I was a city girl. I lived in Lexington, KY, where horses are thoroughbreds and farms are manicured acres of bluegrass enclosed in tidy white fences. As a young, single school-teacher, I ate Egg McMuffins for breakfast and Arby's salad bar for dinner. Popcorn was all I cooked with any certainty of success. I did yard work by paying a boy $5 to mow the patch of grass in front of my duplex. Too lazy to drive three blocks to Foodtown? I borrowed a Coke from the girl next door.

Then, in an odd twist of events which irrefutably proved that God has a sense of humor, I married a wheat farmer from Colfax, WA. To be more precise, he is from an area known as Onecho, twelve miles outside of Colfax. Don't bother looking at your map.

Although Mike tried to convince me there was nothing unusual about our first home, I found it difficult to overlook one small detail: No one lived where we did. There was not another house in sight. As tears gathered in my eyes, he assured me that we had neighbors.

"Where are they?" I cried.

"Well, Aunt Kris lives two hills over that way," he answered, pointing out our bay window.

Great. I felt so much better. Only two hills over.

I used to run to the window and watch our postman drive down the road, just for the comfort of knowing someone else existed. Looking back, I'm surprised I didn't wait by the box and beg to ride along.

In spite of my physical isolation, I did make friends. A few months after moving I called Joan, only to catch her canning cherries.

"What's that?" I asked.

"You know, putting them into jars to eat in the winter."

Ah, yes. My grandmother did that to beans and pickles. So other people did that, too; I thought it was an eccentric habit my grandmother had. I phoned two other friends, who were also canning cherries. Perplexed, I wandered around my small kitchen. How did everyone know to can cherries today? Did I miss an announcement in the paper? Maybe there was a special canning calendar. That must be it, I decided. I would buy one on my next trip to the grange.

I had learned about the grange the hard way. My husband called from the farm one afternoon and asked me to get a couple of fadoogles for the pick-up.

"I don't even know what a fadoogle looks like," I told him.

"No problem," he answered with confidence. "They'll know just what you need."

I nervously approached the counter, feeling out of place without my coveralls and "gimme cap", and asked the man for a couple of fadoogles.

"Do you need 1/2" fadoogles or 5/8" fadoogles?" he asked.

"Umm, I don't know. They're for a pick-up," I offered helpfully.

"Are they going up front on the hobokin case or in the rear on the dunny rods?"

"Umm, he didn't say."

"Do you want copper or aluminum?"

"Umm, copper?"

"These aren't going to be attached to any rubber nokkle hoses, are they? Because if they are, you're better off with aluminum."

"OK, aluminum."

"Are you sure you only want two? Fadoogles usually operate in sets of four. I can sell you two, but you'll have to come back if you need the others."

No, no, anything but that. "I'll take four."

I repeated this scene buying whatzits for the tractor at Jones Truck and Implement and female ends for lingob couplings at the hardware store. Each time my husband assured me "they'll know just what you need" and each time I played twenty questions. I finally concluded that on their coffee breaks the employees make up list of questions to ask unsuspecting wives. They tape the lists to the front of their cash registers for easy reference.

Another occupational hazard of being a farm wife is conversation about the weather. In Lexington, we talked about the weather, too. I might say one of the following:

"Nice day today, isn't it?"

"I hope it doesn't rain."

"I hope it does rain."

"This humidity is killing me."

And after the other party agree/disagreed with me, we talked about something else.

In Colfax, the conversations are more detailed.

"Say, how much rain did you get at your place last night?"

"Oh, just shy of 1/2 inch."

"No kidding? My rain gauge showed about 3/8 inch."

"That so? Well, I had coffee with Bill this morning and he only got 1/4 inch."

"Yeah, but he lives out towards Dusty and they're always drier that we are."

Anyone unfortunate enough to initiate one of these discussions with me quickly discovers that my only rain gauge is a dog dish with a hole in it. The conversation tends to dwindle after that.

Yes, the move has been difficult and, no, I'm still not the perfect farm wife. My apple pie comes frozen in a box with Mrs. Smith's name on it. My attempts at gardening yield bountiful harvests of buttonweed. I don't even like riding in the tractor, much less driving it.

But I am growing, changing, and I like to think I'm impacting my new community, too. One day, iced tea will be an acceptable drink in the winter. One day, people in the Northwest will no longer have to ask where exactly Kentucky is. And, one day, farm wives everywhere will unite with me in saying these immortal words,

"No more trips for fadoogles! We ain't gonna buy them any more!"

Piecing Your Quilt

by SuZanne Curtis
(for my grandmother Anna)

I pick up the hand-me-down pieces—
>   a garden filled with beans, corn tomatoes,
>   a pond where muskrats build dried cattail teepees,
>   baby's breath and blue sweet peas gazing
>   at the distant snow-capped Teton Mountains.
Working rich wheatland earth and broad skies
together to form your border,
>   I long to know your center.

My mother hands me patches of your past.
>   As I stitch them into place, I look for you
in your yard of cosmos, pink and lavender,
>   try to catch your scent with a spring lilac bush
flowering through your open front window.

My aunts checkerwork the rash design of your lost fortune:
>   china, linen, furniture—all stored in the granary
as the homestead was being remodeled.
>   Betraying grass fires razed everything.
"God forsaken country," they say you whispered
>   as you mended your tattered tablecloth.

How can I complete the dark pattern
>   of how that careening car crushed you,
ripping your life away before I knew you,
>   breaking Papa's promise—
he could never take you home to Ireland.

Placing the batting between the layers,
>   I think I hear your whispers,
"Carry me back home, carry me back home."

Colfax and The Devlin Connection

by Leonard Leroy Devlin

Foreword

In the year 1993, I, Leonard Leroy Jones, became Leonard Leroy Devlin. In front of a judge, the process took approximately three minutes; in my own home the process took somewhat longer.

"Why did you do it, for heaven's sake?" Before I could answer she went on: "What have you to gain, especially at *your* age?"

The emphasis on the pronoun I picked up, but decided against raising it as an issue. It was true that I was no longer young. No need to contest that. My older sister was sincere. I needed to reply with the same sincerity. So I tried a different tack.

"Sis, I've been thinking about the name change for over a decade. I feel it's *right*. If you had the time I'd try to explain."

"Try me," she quickly returned.

So, I tried . . .

***

There can be no doubt that the Black Potato Blight was a major disaster for Ireland in the 1840's. Hundreds of thousands starved to death or died of disease. Over a million emigrated to foreign lands, mostly north America. Among the latter were a man, his wife, and their teenage son. Boarding a slave-trade sailing vessel now carrying Irish emigrants, they left the west coast town of Sligo, bound for America. On a vessel with few sanitary facilities and even less food than on their famine-ridden island, deaths were commonplace. Before the trip was over, both parents were gone, victims of what was known simply as "ship fever." Only the young lad would set foot on the promised land of America. It was he, weak and alone as he was, who would carry the name Devlin to a fresh start in a new land.

Interrupting the story, I stated, with some sense of elation, "That lad, Sis, was our great grandfather, Patrick Devlin!" Of course she knew this and I knew that she knew it. Her quick nod sent me on with my story.

The Devlins were, in better times, people of the soil, farmers with small dairies. That was perhaps the reason why young Patrick tarried no longer than absolutely necessary in Boston before heading west. He made his way beyond the Great Lakes, to the territory of Wisconsin which was open to settlement. There was work to be done and he soon found employment, working for sod-busters at first and then starting a homestead of his own. There also, he met and fell in love with a girl from a neighboring county in Ireland, Katherine Clark by name, from County Louthe. When she accepted his proposal of marriage, they began a family. Two boys came first, Edward and John. The girls, Bridget and Margaret, would come later. From all that we can gather, the Devlins were a close-knit family: they stood together through good times—and these were good times—and bad. The bad times were to come with the Confederate cannon aimed at Fort Sumter in 1861.

Patrick Devlin had come to love this new land; he was now ready to sacrifice his life in its defense. When President Lincoln called for 75,000 volunteers "to safeguard the properties of the Federal Government," Patrick was among the first to enlist. His unit? The Wisconsin 12th Infantry Regiment. Under its battle flags he would serve, first close to Washington, D.C., and later in campaigns across the deep south. He would emerge unscathed after four long deadly years. Sadly, his son, young Edward Devlin, would not. His story is an interesting one.

At this point I once again hesitated in my story telling. I turned to my sister Regis and asked, "How much of Grandfather's tale have you heard?" By her eyes I knew, not enough! So I pushed on . . .

As history recites, the great Civil War began with oratory and fanfare, drums and bugles—a great show, a great adventure was about to begin! In both the north and the south preparations were made for a short, glorious interlude, success coming swiftly with victory to "their" side. Perhaps the contagion that swept most of the young men of Wisconsin into the Federal forces was what prompted Edward Devlin to try the same. He was certain that his father was marching away to great glory. With equal certainty he felt he was missing out on the adventure of a lifetime. He had to be a part of it. With determination that was uniquely a mark of his character, he ran away to a neighboring town, enlisted as a color bearer or drummer boy, lying about his age and surname. To foil a possible search by his mother he took the common name of Jones. Suffice it to say, it worked. His family lost all track of him. Like U.S. Grant, with Forts Henry and Donelson under his belt, in 1862, Edward Jones "moved south" into the midst of history.

At this juncture my listener interrupted my story telling. "Do you honestly mean to say that an eleven-year-old boy would be accepted by the military?" She was totally incredulous.

For just a moment I was amused. From our latter-day point of view such a scheme as my grandfather had concocted truly seemed unbelievable. Slowly, for her sake (and, to tell the truth, partly my own) I recited instances where youths as tender as nine were accepted, by volunteer regiments especially. In the "euphoria" atmosphere of the days before Bull Run, no one expected to see true battle or be away from home longer than ninety days. History would prove them dreadfully wrong . . .

What we know with certainty is that the great battle of Shiloh in April 1862 marked the beginning of an awareness that this war would require many such battles. A long, brutal conflict was in store. Thousand would die in this conflict, as many to dysentery as to war wounds. It is in this nebulous period of campaign after campaign (most of which in the drive for Vicksburg ended in defeat and frustration) that young Edward Jones disappeared. In later years he would not speak of it. Only his unknown sickness that would mark all his later years remains a certainty.

It is well to note true history here: Grant was to cross the mighty Mississippi, corduroy his way through the vaporous, sickly bayous and eventually return to the river south of "impregnable Vicksburg." In this period, Edward, sick in body and perhaps also in spirit, was taken captive. Louisiana was effectively cut off, her cotton value-less. With an invitation to settle upriver Brazil (offered by Emperor Pedro II) a group of wealthy landholders sailed south to the Amazon—taking a sickly Edward Jones with them. They would establish, they believed, a new kingdom of cotton. The would name this enterprise "The New America."

"Why," I could almost hear my listener ask, "would they take along a sickly boy on such an arduous undertaking?"

One possible answer lies in a large gravestone still standing from that era. Today this area of Brazil retains its pre-Civil War heritage: it is not called the planned "New America" but rather "Americana." A gravestone there designates the final resting place of a large land-holder by the name of—yes—Jones! One can only surmise that the family took pity on a desperately ill lad from the north. (Enough of the guessing, but, in point of fact, that is all that we know.)

Cotton was known to be labor intensive, and slavery was not tol-erated in Brazil. A cotton kingdom was a desperate, if courageous venture. It was doomed from its inception. But for Edward Jones this was a time for regaining his health. Working for his room and board, he grew stronger as the years crawled by. When the venture collapsed, he was freed. With new-found determination he made his way across the Andes and down to a port on the Peruvian coast. There he was able to find a working passage on a vessel headed for the fabled city of San Francisco. The year was 1865, the month, August.

The authorities of the "City by the Bay" quarantined the entire crew. The cause? Cholera! For six long weeks, or as he would put it, "the hottest months of his life!" he was kept aboard the old sailing vessel in the harbor. Released at last, he hurried north to the beauti-ful valley of the Umpqua, in Oregon. There, under the tutelage of an uncle who had come out west in the glory days of '49, he learned the timbering trade. He took quickly to this new way of life. Regrettably, the weather of this coastal territory quickly brought back his illness. With the winters mild but very wet, he faced a hard choice: move or die slowly. He moved.

North on the Willamette, the bustling city of Portland needed carpenters and Edward quickly found employment. He liked the city but found dampness again left him ill. When times of a warmer, drier clime east of the Cascades reached him, he determined, then and there, that he would not rest until he found a land that would restore his health. In the spring of 1868, Edward Thomas Devlin-Jones rode into the rising sun—and east of the mountains.

As he would later tell daughter Edith, the Yakima country was not appealing—too many Indians and too many rocks! It was not until he had crossed the Columbia and the Snake Rivers that he would see what he instinctively knew was his personal promised land. Edith would relate, to those of us who came in later generations, that Edward found an endless view of grass as "tall as the belly of his horse." Also, that fine May morning, the breeze moved the grass "in waves just like the ones he had seen on his voyage north from Peru!" This would be his home, the land where he would build his private "Empire of Sheep."

It must be understood by the reader of these lines, as it was to my sister, that with the coming of peace in the land came a great surge of settlers heading west. It was a land of promise to everyone. To an area where the fairgrounds now stand came a party of Southerners under the leadership of William Holt. They gave their name to the fertile strip of land called "Rebel Flat."

Another party, this one from the north, settled a more densely timbered area just a few miles west. The name this party chose? Of course, "Union Flat." Its leader? James Ewart. With him came the man who would become the father of Colfax, James Perkins. With great hopes he began the platting of a town at the confluence of the north and south Palouse Rivers. The scenario was set: all that was needed was a mill for the homes for what would surely be a great city! Hezekiah Hollingsworth, with his water-powered mill, would solve that problem—if only for a little while. It is enough to say that Edward Jones would find himself as sawyer in that first old mill in 1869.

It is in these years that the Colfax Connection becomes apparent. Despite all human effort, the erratic and often short-lived stream flows made the Hollingsworth mill inadequate. In these years, four months was about all he could coax out of the water-powered mill.

To the owner this meant near failure; to Edward it meant changing from sawing logs to erecting every edifice human needs might warrant. Homes, of course, came first, but barns and businesses were soon needed. In his spare time he methodically searched for a homestead. It had to meet his every requirement for he intended to raise sheep. And, in the end, he settled on the western side of Colfax, a horseshoe ring of hills around a broad expanse of flat, hills that were his for the grazing—the place we now call home.

It is in this brief period that he met the lass he had always sought, a diminutive (4'11") native of Indiana, and later Missouri. By all measurements she must have appeared woefully unsuited to the wild untamed west. Edward obviously saw more than most: he courted her and the two were married on November 1, 1873, in Colfax.

Postscript

In the years that followed, the Devlin connection expanded. When word reached Wisconsin that Edward Devlin (now Jones) was alive in Colfax, the family moved west to join him. The Codd brothers, Patrick and William, installed a new steam-powered mill, with a mill pond to keep logs fresh winter or summer. (The pond was located on the site of the present Excell Foods Store on, naturally, Mill Street.) In point of fact, the Codd boys did more than that: they met and married the Devlin sisters, Bridget and Margaret. Father Patrick and Mother Katherine would have their family together again for the happy wedding. The only flaw in this scenario? No one would carry on the Devlin name. But more importantly, no one would ever know his true roots.

Almost a century after Patrick died, a great grandson tried to remedy that—the reason I changed my name to Devlin.

END OF THE WORLD (PART 3)

by Vickie L. Cook

Clinging to the sink in my bathroom. Door closed and locked.
Remembering your assault and looking for bruises in the mirror.
No black and blue spots anywhere that I can see. Except for my
    eyes.
Okay . . . so don't look at them or into them.
Oh! Silly me, I forgot . . . words only leave bruises on the soul.

THE TIGER AND THE PARROT

by Alysia Herr (age 7)

Once upon a time there was a tiger and a parrot. The tiger thought it was lunch, but no it wasn't, it was dinner. The tiger said, "I think I will have a bird." So he set off to find one. He saw a parrot. "Yummy, I just love parrot," said the tiger. So he crept up and jumped into the air. The parrot flew away laughing. The tiger said, "I'll get that bird no matter what she does. I think I'll make a trap. I'll put bird seed on a little net and then I'll hold onto this rope and when parrot walks into the net I will pull the rope and get that bird." So he waited and waited. Then he got so tired he went to sleep. The parrot crept into the net and gobbled the bird seed down. When the tiger woke up he saw that the seeds were gone. "Oh, I give up," said the tiger, "I'll find another thing to eat."

A COOK'S DILEMMA

by Della Evans

I've spent a lot of years
In the kitchen
Cooking for a crowd
Most of the time, a crew of men.

But now when I set the table
There's just plates for two
And yet enough food
To feed yesteryear's crew.

Those old habits that are with you
Are so hard to break
When you start to peel,
Mix and bake.

Unless I make eight loaves
My Bread won't turn out the way it should
And that's the way it is with everything
If my culinary concoctions are to be tasty and good.

When it's always been
A ranch crew you've fed
It's automatic to plan meals
With beef, vegies, potatoes and bread.

Now the doctor tells me
I shouldn't do that
That I should put
Fish and chicken in our diet.

So I go to the freezer
And get a chicken out
Then for a week I learn

What innovative cooking is all about.
For you can fry up
A piece or two
Then the rest goes into salads,
Sandwiches or stew.

Boy, that gets tiresome
And what a bore
Just how do you manage
To eat chicken any more.

So I guess my answer
Is to get another dog and cat
Then they could eat all the left-overs
And they can get big and fat.

SOMEWHERE THE SUN ALWAYS SHINES

by Ralph E. Morgan

Editor's note: Ralph Morgan died in 1970. He was the son Mr. and Mrs. Al Morgan of Rosalia. In the second grade he was struck with muscular dystrophy which he battled for over 15 years before succumbing to its effects. We are grateful to his mother, Evelyn Morgan, for providing us these contributions and allowing us to publish them as a part of this anthology. "Somewhere the Sun Always Shines" was written in 1967. Ralph's other contribution, "Howdy Gal!" was written in 1970.

Ryan "Irish" O'Connor walked briskly across the famed UCLA campus. It was something of a tradition in the O'Connor family to attend this particular university and Irish was no exception. From as far back as he could remember, it had always been his big dream and now it was a reality. Now twenty-three years old, he was completing his final semester of college and doing exceptionally well, in fact, he would graduate sixth in his engineering class. Physically, Ryan was in top condition and he carried his 6'1", 190 lb. frame with the grace and ease of a natural-born athlete. His blue eyes and blonde hair, with an impish-looking tuft over each corner of his forehead, only added to his already personable appearance. The rush to the classroom was of importance for he had heard from fellow students that this particular instructor barred all late arrivals and Ryan was taking no chances.

As he approached the foreign languages building, Ryan met several friends, together they continued on to the classroom. While chatting jokingly with the group, he wandered about the room, checking various notices on the board. With this task complete, he took a seat near the front of the room and prepared for the upcoming class. Despite his heavy schedule in the engineering department, he had managed to spare a few extra hours each week to dabble in his hobby of foreign languages. Ryan was especially fond of the languages of Eastern Europe. The warning buzzer rang, soon class would begin.

The instructor entered the room with all the eagerness of a man in a hurry; he was followed by an attractive, green-eyed blonde. The straggler was lucky, a few seconds more and she would have missed her class. Irish was strangely attracted to this girl for some odd reason and he kept his eyes riveted to her every move. Could it be, he thought to himself, was this lovely girl the skinny, freckle-faced Macy Lynn O'Brian of his childhood? He thought back to the wonderful times he and "Mac," as he affectionately remembered her, had had as children. They used to walk through the Los Angeles hills to their special spot overlooking a beautiful green meadow and its silver-blue stream winding to the river. They had set for hours under the powerful, lone oak and laughed and talked and they had promised each other that someday they would marry. He remembered the sad parting they had to make when her parents moved back East to Boston when he was thirteen and she eleven. It seemed so long ago and yet, it seemed like yesterday. Ryan's daydreaming was cut short by the sharp voice of the instructor.

"Mr. O'Connor! If you would care to turn your attention to the front of the room, would you do us the honor of translating this sentence, please!"

"Ah. Er. Y-y-yes s-s-sir," he stammered and he proceeded to translate the sentence from German to English. He then lapsed to his memories. Again the booming voice of his instructor pierced the air.

"Mr. O'Connor! This is a classroom. You are here to learn! Sir, is that understood?"

"S-s-sorry S-s-sir," Ryan replied and the class exploded with good-natured laughter. And so continued the remainder of the period, the booming voice of the instructor, the embarrassment of Irish O'Connor, and the laughter of his friends. The bell rang and a big sigh of relief came from the red-faced young man.

Still wondering about Macy Lynn, he bent over to accumulate his belongings, looking up, he noticed that the green-eyed blonde was staring at him through tearful eyes and smiling. Only they remained in the room.

"Irish," she said hopefully, "is that really you?"

"Mac! Mac!" Ryan shouted happily and rushed to greet her only to succeed in tripping over his usually sure feet, falling over two chairs and sending papers, pencils, books, and notebooks flying through the air.

"You always were the graceful one!" she teased playfully. "What have you heard from your feet lately?"

Irish grinned sheepishly and retorted, "Would you believe that I received an 'A' in dancing class? A 'B'? A 'C'? How about an incomplete?" and they both laughed heartily while Ryan recovered his possessions.

Classes for the remainder of the day were suddenly forgotten as they walked hand in hand out of the foreign languages building and onto the campus. Both were talking rapidly, laughing about the "old days" and the people they used to know. Reaching a nearby grocer, whom Irish knew personally, they secured enough food and Pepsi for an afternoon picnic. Task completed, they walked over to the parking lot and piled their belongings into Ryan's late model sedan and away they drove. Their destination was the large hill overlooking the meadow on which they so wonderfully passed the time as children. A forty-five minute drive from campus brought them to the desired location. They hiked to the top and spread a blanket beneath the lone oak, placing the food and soft drinks on one half, themselves upon the other. The two examined the ancient tree, yes, it was still there after all those years. . . a roughly drawn heart with the names "Mac" & "Irish" carved inside. It brought back many memories to the young couple.

The day passed slowly for Ryan and Macy. It seemed to them that they were alone in the world and that time had reversed itself to another day many years ago, on that same hill, the same two people.

Dusk found them in much the same position that they had maintained throughout the greater part of the afternoon; Mac sitting with her back propped against the old oak tree and Irish with his head nestled in her lap. Mostly they talked, but often they would merely gaze into each other's eyes and words were unnecessary. Evening came and still the young couple remained upon the hill. The pale moon crept up into the vast sky, the stars sparkled brightly. From the meadow below, they could hear the beautiful but haunting melody of the night.

"Mac, do you remember that silly promise we made as kids, the one about waiting for each other?" Irish asked shyly.

"I didn't think it was silly," Mac whispered seriously.

"Mac."

"Yes, darling?"

"Mac. . . Mac, will you marry me? I know this is sudden and it almost seems unreal, like a dream, but I can't help it, it has always been you." he said.

"Oh yes, yes, Irish, darling, I love you very much," she said softly. "I've waited so long to hear those words."

"I graduate July 30th and it will take several months to find a place and become settled in my new job. Would October 19th be too soon?"

"October 19th, I will be Mrs. Ryan Patrick 'Irish' O'Connor." Macy sighed and then kissed him softly. "We'll always be together."

"Yes, Macy—always." The gentle man kissed his future wife with tenderness and she wept because she was so very happy.

The following months passed quickly. Ryan completed the semester successfully and graduated with honors. He had several opportunities to assume positions with such established and powerful firms as RCA, Zenith, General Electric, and Westinghouse. Surprisingly enough, he passed up all offers. Instead, Irish and his two best friends, Bob Pateros & Mike Rhodes, sought out and secured positions with Morgan Electronics, a small, but fast-growing and prominent firm in Los Angeles. The reasons were quite clear to the eager, young trio; a small firm offered more opportunities for advancement. The starting salary for each of the young men was $710 per month. Ryan would begin his marriage and his career upon solid ground.

The wedding day was here and Ryan was shaking as does any good groom when it comes his day to take the final step. The drive to the little parish church in the San Fernando Valley seemed to take hours. The wedding would be small and simple with both sides of parents, grandparents, and a few chosen friends attending. To Ryan, Macy was the most beautiful bride in the world. He stood in awe as he watched her glide gracefully down the aisle to his side. The Nuptial Mass passed smoothly. After the newlyweds received the congratulations from well-wishers, they rushed to the car and drove off into a new world.

The honeymoon was a wondrous three weeks affair in the beautiful Pacific Northwest. They hiked through hills, explored caves, rode horses down the ancient trails, and rediscovered all those things that the years had erased. The marriage had a lovely beginning and the added advantage of a firm foundation that would last forever. They vowed to return to the northern paradise for a second honeymoon.

Like every first year of wedded bliss, there were many adjustments to be made, the O'Connor's family was no exception. There were spats over her cooking, the bills, and the bad habits of both husband and wife. Yet with each argument came new understanding and increased love and devotion. They were young, very much in love, and truly happy.

While Mac attended to household chores, Ryan, Bob and Mike worked well as a team in the Morgan Corporation. The three men were working on a new system for one of the company's space projects and if the system proved successful, it would mean a small raise to the hard-working trio.

One afternoon, while Irish was at work, Macy made a special trip to a downtown doctor. Twenty-one months of wedded bliss had brought the oncoming of their first-born. The doctor confirmed Macy's belief, she was in her second month. Happily, she returned home to plan some impish way of breaking the news to Ryan. She had it! She would wait until dinner was over and he was deeply engrossed in the evening newspaper before she would spring the glad tidings.

"Honey! Honey, I'm home!"

"I'm in the kitchen, dear!"

"What's going on, are we having guests? Why the fancy food? Mmmmm, my favorite dishes! Out with it, Tiger, how much was the new dress? Good grief! My car, you smashed my car! I have it, you're so overwhelmed with the Master's charm, talent, and good looks that you just can't help showing your deep appreciation, huh? You may rise slave."

"Yes, darling," and she smiled at him impishly.

The evening meal was filled with conversation concerning the day's activities. Ryan told her of the progress they were making on the project and that with luck, it would be completed within the next four months. Ryan also told her of his hopes and plans for the building of a new home upon completion of the project. The house came as a perfect surprise to Macy. Their apartment was fine, but a home of their own! With the meal completed, Irish retired to the den and the newspaper; Mac to the kitchen and the dishes. Twenty minutes later, she rejoined her husband.

"Did you have a hard day, dear?"

"Hmmmm," was the reply.

"Nice day, wasn't it, darling?"

"Hmmmm," was the reply.

"Honey, we're going to have a baby."

"Hmmmm," was again the reply.

"Sweetheart, did you hear me?"

"Yes, dear. . .Good grief! Mickey Mantle hit five home runs!" Then the full impact of his wife's remark sank in. "WE'RE GOING TO HAVE A BABY!" He jumped up and once more his usual sure-footedness left him and he tripped over the foot stool, sprawling to the floor. Quickly, he jumped to his feet, but only to go flying over a slippery rag rug. This time he just lay there laughing and half moaning in feigned agony. Of course, Ryan knew of the possibility, but the news made him ecstatic.

Macy laughed heartily over her husband's sudden awkwardness and silently recalled the day they had rediscovered each other in the classroom and in his haste to greet her had met a similar fate. "Easy does it, Irish," she said and as she knelt beside him, he messed her hair playfully.

"Darling, I'm so happy," he whispered as a sudden moistness filled his twinkling eyes. "I'm so happy!" He hugged her tightly.

Later that evening they walked over to their small parish church to offer a small prayer of thanks. They lit one candle and returned home happily. The next seven months passed quickly for the O'Connor's Clan.

Birth, like its counterpart death, is no respecter of time. At 3:00 a.m., July 24th, Macy woke in sudden pain, the time had come. Calmly, she dressed and then woke Ryan gently. "It's time, darling."

"Mmmmm . . . tell the boss that I'm sick," and he rolled over and was deep in sleep.

"No darling, it's time for the baby."

Like every good, all-American father for the first time, he took it with all of the grace of an earthquake. "B-B-Baby!" He bolted from his bed and they were off to Saint Rose Hospital.

If the drive to the hospital was nerve-wracking, then the waiting was even more unbearable. Back and forth he paced. He read, he paced, munched candy bars, paced, gulped soft drinks, paced and just when he thought that he couldn't stand it any longer, news came.

"Mr. O'Connor, it's a boy, nine pounds, ten ounces."

"WHOOEE!" he shouted. "IT'S A BOY!"

"Please, Mr. O'Connor! This IS a hospital. Quiet is appreciated," the nurse reprimanded.

"I'm s-s-sorry," he said as the crimson rose to his face.

"Mr. O'Connor," said the nurse, "it's a beautiful baby and you have every right to be proud, but could you do so in a more controlled manner? You may see your wife now, but only for a few moments. She's fine but needs rest."

Irish walked swiftly to his wife's room, opened the door and walked softly to her side, took her hands in his and whispered in her ear, "I love you, Mac."

"Is the baby all right?"

"Yes, Honey, the Rams will have another great fullback someday." Ryan winked and kissed her tenderly.

The child was christened in the name of his father: Ryan Patrick. Happiness reigned supreme in the "House of O'Connor."

Four years passed from the time of their first-born and Lil' Ryan now had a little sister, Margaret Marie, and a little brother, Kelly Brian. The two older children took after their mother, but Kelly was his father's son. With the eagerness and curiosity that only the young seem to possess in such huge quantities, the three were into anything and everything. Despite the big lawn, Lil' Ryan could always be found in the nearest dirt pile, Margaret in the kitchen, knee-deep in pots and pans, and Kelly was forever being escorted away from the toilet bowl. When bedtime rolled around, Macy and Ryan would breathe a sigh of relief.

All was well. They owned a beautiful ranch in the San Fernando Valley, their marriage was fine, the children were happy and healthy, Ryan's job was running smoothly, but most of all, they were bound on all sides by love. The time seemed perfect for a second honeymoon. They would make the necessary arrangements as soon as

Macy and the children returned from a week's visit with her parents in Boston.

It was a clear and crisp April morning as Ryan helped prepare his family for the journey back East. Packed, they drove to the airport. The parting was one of mixed emotions, happy over the prospect of a pleasant reunion, sad because this was to be their first major separation. They vowed to make it their last.

Ryan kissed his children, ruffled their hair playfully, and told them to take good care of their mother. He turned to his wife and bade her farewell. He held her tightly and whispered in her ear, "I love you, Mac. Come home soon."

"Yes, darling, soon. I love you."

Ryan watched as his family boarded the huge jet plane. He remained at the gate until they had flown out of sight and then he drove off to work.

Mike and Bob were standing near a window when Ryan's car pulled into the parking lot.

"Ryan will really miss his family!"

"You're right, Mike, he looks lost already."

Ryan strolled across the parking lot and into the building. He spotted his friends and went over to greet them. "Good morning! Are you ready for another session? There's nothing like trial and error to begin your day."

"I agree. This new project is twice as bad as our first and second ones," Bob said.

"Did you get your family off all right this morning?" Asked Mike.

"Sure did, Mike. Our place won't seem the same without the kids running in and out. This could be a long week!" The remainder of the day flew quickly by. That evening Ryan returned to the dark, deserted house. The quiet seemed strange. He prepared several sandwiches and entered the den to watch television. An hour elapsed and Irish became restless, he turned to the newspaper, but he couldn't concentrate. Finally, he went to bed.

The following morning he ate a light breakfast and drove to work. He met Bob and Mike near the front office and joined them as they walked into the plant. "Since the ranch is rather deserted, you should both come on out and stay a few days. It's really great out there this time of year!"

"Sounds like a great idea," they replied. After work, Ryan followed his friends to their apartment and then he drove them out to his home in the San Fernando Valley. The first evening they treated themselves to a huge steak dinner and later on they took an evening swim in Ryan's pool.

For the next five days, the trio enjoyed a semi-reunion. They got in a few afternoons of golf or fishing, watched several evening baseball games, took in several movies, visited a few night clubs, and slept very little as a result.

Saturday morning the trio drove a rented truck to a neighboring ranch. Between the three men they chose two ponies and two puppies for Ryan's children. The animals were a homecoming present. Returning to Ryan's ranch, they unloaded the newly acquired stock and then headed to the house for lunch. Later that same afternoon, Ryan drove Bob and Mike back to their apartment. They all agreed that in some future time they would "bach" it again. Ryan returned to the ranch, fed the animals, straightened and cleaned the house, ate a light snack, and lay down on the sofa for a nap. An hour passed before he was awakened by the phone. "Hello, O'Connor's residence."

"Hello, darling."

"Macy, how are you? Is everything all right? How are the children? Are you enjoying your visit?"

"We're fine and we've had a wonderful week. I miss you, Honey! How have you gotten along?"

"I had Bob and Mike out for a few days and we had a good time, too, but I missed you very much. Tell the children that I have a surprise for them. Give your folks my love. When will you be coming home, Honey?"

"Our plane leaves in several hours, we'll be home 7:00 a.m. your time tomorrow morning. It'll be so good to be home again! I love you."

"I love you! I'll be waiting at the gate, have a good trip home." Ryan blew a kiss to his wife and then hung up his receiver. Ryan whistled happily and returned to a few unfinished tasks, checked the puppies and fed them again, grabbed another quick snack for himself, watched several of his favorite television programs, and then went to bed.

Just before the break of dawn a heavy storm fell upon the Los Angeles area. Ryan tossed wildly in his sleep and he had a dream, a terrible dream. He saw a plane pitched about by heavy winds, lose altitude, and then crash into a side of a mountain. Ryan awoke suddenly. He was in a cold sweat and shaking badly. A few minutes passed before he could calm himself. A cold dark, and foreboding feeling lurked within his body. Ryan slept lightly until the rude ringing of the phone brought him back to reality.

"Mr. O'Connor," asked a solemn voice, "this is Mr. Wakefield of United Airlines. Would you please come down to my office as soon as possible?"

Ryan dressed. Thoughts of all kinds raced through his mind—was his dream a reality? He erased the idea and sent a quick prayer on the behalf of his family's safety. Reaching the airport, he located Mr. Wakefield and they walked to his office. Ryan took a seat while Mr. Wakefield moved about restlessly.

"Mr. O'Connor, news has reached my office that our 7:00 a.m. flight has been lost. Our people are at the sight of the crash and they have confirmed beyond doubt that there were no survivors. I am very sorry, please let me know if there is anything that I can possible do."

The loss of his family stunned him. His stomach knotted severely, he sat in numbed silence for several moments. He summoned enough strength to thank Mr. Wakefield for the kindness he had performed.

The sun was shining brightly and the sound of children's laughter filled the air as Ryan walked to his car. He sat silently for a few moments, looked towards the heavens and bitterly cursed his Maker for the loss of his family. Irish drove to the nearest bar, but found little relief. He left the bar and walked through the streets of the city until dawn. Several days later he attended funeral services for his family. His friends tried to comfort him, but failed. The heaviness within his heart was unbearable, he was unable to cry.

Ryan returned to work the following week in hopes of burying his grief in his job. It was to no avail, he couldn't concentrate on the project. Finally, O'Connor requested an indefinite leave of absence from Morgan Electronics. He invited Bob and Mike to live at his ranch until he returned. They accepted. His plans made, a bitter and desolate man left his past in Los Angeles to wander the earth in loneliness.

After seven months of travel in the United States, Ryan boarded a plane bound for Salzburg, Austria. Midway through the flight a severe storm struck and memories of a crash haunted Ryan's mind. He broke into a cold sweat, fear gripped his body and he wanted to cry out, but held back. Badly shaken, partly in shock, O'Connor stepped off the plane at the Salzburg air terminal, passed through customs, and walked to a small hotel to rest. Restlessness set in and he left word at the desk that he would return that evening.

All afternoon Ryan wandered through the green valley, along the winding Salzach River and into the hills. He glanced towards the sky and noticed storm clouds overhead. Upon walking several hundred yards further, Ryan tired and stopped to rest. He looked around, everything was still, even the birds had stopped their noisy chattering. Something had frightened them. He located a heavy wooden club and listened intensively. Several yards away he could see the movement of bushes. Carefully Ryan stalked closer. The movement stopped and its place came the whimpering of a small child. Ryan parted the brush and found a little boy sitting in a clump of late-blooming wild flowers. Thinking that there must be adults nearby, Ryan called out—no answer. He called out again, still no one answered him. The boy must have wandered off and had become lost, he concluded. He stared at the child as bitter memories filled his heart and in rage he cursed God for the loss of his own children. Still cursing, Ryan turned, walked away and left the child behind.

Several minutes later, he returned to the child's side, cradled the boy in his arms and sought shelter as a heavy rain began to pour down. The storm was gnawing at Ryan's strength, he was becoming weak and dizzy. He stumbled and groped his way through the darkness. He saw a flickering light on the hill above him. Upon finding the passageway, he climbed the ancient stone steps—only a few feet more. Reaching the door, Ryan knocked with his last remaining strength. It seemed like years before the door swung open. He handed the child to a woman and collapsed to the floor. He was near death. The woman summoned help and they carried Ryan to a bedroom, removed his wet clothing and put him to bed.

The place into which Ryan had stumbled or was guided, he

would later discover, was Nonnberg. Twelve hundred years before, Saint Erentrudis had founded the old Abbey, the first abbey of the Benedictine Nuns to be so founded north of the Alps. It was a place of unearthly beauty.

For the next three nights and nearly four days, Ryan uttered many bitter curses as he tossed and turned in his delirium. One of the nuns was near his side at all times, bathing him with sponge baths in hopes of curbing his terrible fever. At the same time, one nun remained in the chapel to pray for the ill man and his soul. The procedure continued around the clock.

Midway through the fourth afternoon, Ryan beheld a vision, but it seemed distant and not at all like his dream of the crash. This time he saw his wife and children smiling and waving down at him. They seemed unusually happy. As quickly as the vision appeared, it vanished. Ryan would never see the vision again. Thirty minutes later, a nun discovered that the burning fever had broken, she said a prayer of thanks. The weakened man slept soundly for the first time.

Upon waking the following morning, Ryan discovered one of the nuns gazing down upon him. She was young, attractive and blue-eyed. Her smile was warm and friendly and her face seemed so full of love. The nun talked to him softly and explained the happenings of the past four days. She told him that the boy was fine and was anxious to see him, but that he would have to wait until Ryan had gained more strength.

That afternoon the door to Ryan's room opened slowly. The child paused until Ryan motioned him to enter. O'Connor grinned and lifted the boy gently onto his lap. He sat on his lap for several moments and then flung his chubby arms around his friend's neck and hugged him tightly. Bewildered at first, he sat motionless, then, for the first time since the loss of his family, tears streamed down Ryan's face. The bitterness and hatred which had been stored within for many months had finally found an outlet, he was free. Ryan held the child tightly. The small lad reached up with tiny fingers and brushed away the remaining tears. The happenings of the afternoon had drained much of Ryan's strength, exhausted, he was overcome by sleep. A passing nun looked in on the pair, finding them asleep, she smiled and walked on.

Four weeks later, Ryan had recovered sufficiently enough to

leave the abbey. He returned to the small hotel in Salzburg. Each day Ryan rented a horse-drawn sleigh and drove to Nonnberg to visit the Sisters and Eric, the small boy. In the meantime, Salzburg authorities searched vainly for the abandoned child's parents.

Another month elapsed and Ryan continued to make his daily trips to the abbey. He would take Eric on walks through snow-covered woods and meadows. They would sled down slopes and skate merrily over the icy ponds. When Ryan wasn't outdoors with the child, he would be inside rough-housing or reading to him. They were growing closer together each day, but the time on Ryan's visa was running out.

Eric wasn't the only one with whom Ryan spent a great deal of time. He spent many wonderful hours with the blue-eyed Maria, the young novice of the first morning. They talked of many things, including the loss of his family. Ryan's hatred and bitterness had vanished along with his vision of his family. He told her of his home in the beautiful San Fernando Valley of California and of the happiness he had known there. He was truly grateful for what time he had with his family. He believed himself to be a very fortunate man. He was at peace once more.

Two months more elapsed and with it came the expiration date of Ryan's visa. Forty-eight hours later, Ryan would have to leave his friends. It would be hard to say farewell to the people who had done so much for him. His hardest task would come when he had to part with Eric. He wondered how he would explain to a three-year-old boy that even though he loved him, he must leave him behind. Ryan talked with the Reverend Mother of Nonnberg and arranged for the boy to be well cared for. He hoped that it wouldn't be long before he could send for the child.

Parting with the Sisters of the abbey seemed easy compared to the ordeal he endured with the child. Eric could not understand why his friend must go away, big tears flowed down his cheeks. Maria had to restrain the crying child as Ryan drove away. Several hundred feet later, Ryan stopped to take one last look at the ancient abbey. His friends remained on the steps watching his departure and waving. The child continued to cry unceasingly. Ryan completed his journey into Salzburg with tear-stained eyes. Reaching the telegraph office, he sent the following message to Mike and Bob:

Ryan O'Connor
March 2nd.
Salzburg, Austria

Mike Rhodes and Bob Pateros
4586 Irish Drive
Los Angeles, California

Mike & Bob:
    I'm coming home.

                    Ryan.

UNTITLED POEM 94

by Jeff Lageson

My stoicism is a facade
My emotions are really storms
    Logic
    A facade of cold decisions
    Amidst a swirl of hot options
    Pleasure
Will I order a pizza or not?

DEAR FREDDIE

by MacKenzie Raye Van Cleef

Dear Freddie,

How could you? How could you go off and leave us like that? What are we supposed to do now? Don't you know we can't go on without you? Don't you? Not a one of us. Not one. And most especially me.

I don't want to do this. I don't want to face a future without you in it. Didn't I support you enough? Didn't I love you enough? What did I do wrong?

You left me. Without telling anyone, you left. How could you do that to me? To us? DAMN YOU!

Why didn't you tell us something was wrong? We would have loved you. I would have loved you. No matter what.

You were there when I needed you. When the beatings finally got unbearable and the touching, (oh, God, the touching) got to where I felt like I wanted to die, you were there.

You sang me to sleep through my pain and tears and the loneliness. Now who will sing me to sleep? WHO Freddie? Who will sing me to sleep tonight?

***

I move through the motions of caring for my family. I fix dinner, wash clothes and clean house, but I'm not really here. Everyone is walking on egg shells, afraid I'll burst into tears again at any given moment.

I just can't believe you're gone. Just can't believe it. I think I'm through crying for now. I'm still numb. I feel like I'm in a bad dream and at any moment I'll wake up. Then everyone around me will laugh at the way I've been acting.

What I want to do, besides cry, is scream. At you, at God, at the whole damn world.

***

I received a package from Jacky today. I don't dare open it. I don't dare not. Jacky's been doing a bang-up job running the fan club lately, you would be really proud of her.

It's been two months since that God-awful day when I got the call from my sister that sent my life into a tailspin. I suppose I should be grateful for her efforts, really. Not only was that day one of the only two times Teresa said she loved me, it showed that she was thinking of me.

She called me, concern and compassion in her voice, and asked if I was watching T.V.

"No."

"Are you sitting down?"

"No, why?"

"I wanted you to hear this from someone who loves you—"

"Teres, what are you babbling on about, you're starting to scare me. Is it mom? Has something happened to mom—"

"No, no, no, it has nothing to do with mom. I'm watching MTV and they just had that Kurt Loder guy, you know, the one that does the news, anyway, he just came on and announced that Freddie Mercury, lead singer of the rock group Queen—" and I knew you were gone.

I screamed, cried and basically pitched a fit. Michael (dear sweet love, Michael), wrapped his arms around me and held me while I sobbed.

He gently broke the news to our children, all of whom liked Queen as well, and most of whom burst into tears at once. It's three bloody days before Thanksgiving. Three bloody days! What do I have to be thankful for now?

***

The package is actually from the fan club. It's hard to believe it's been eight years since I became a member. It seems like a lifetime ago.

With foreboding I tear open the envelope. Again I cry. There, staring back at me, is a picture of you in funny clothes and makeup. Printed underneath the photograph are the words: IN MEMORIUM, and under that, FREDDIE MERCURY: 5 September 1946-24 November 1991.

Inside is a letter from Jacky, talking about your service and telling us how you wanted your final days to be. Your parents added a letter, thanking the fans for all of the cards and flowers. I never even sent anything. I was too busy hurting and denying to think of anyone else. Brian wrote, for the band, saying that you carried the heavy burden of your declining health by yourself until almost the end.

Jesus, Freddie, why? You could have told us. We would have been there for you. You took that away from us. You gave us no time to prepare; no time to tell you how we felt about you; no time to say good-bye. I hate you for that. I will always hate you for that.

***

The one year anniversary of your passing is here. I really don't want to face it. I miss you so much. Jacky says she is working on finding a spot where a memorial can be placed. I'd rather have you.

***

Michael and I are talking. He is concerned that, after three years, I am still grieving, and he is worried over how angry I get whenever we discuss your illness and death.

It just makes me so mad! You had everything to live for and no reason to die. Michael asks me if I thought you did it on purpose, the dying I mean.

"You're plum crazy," I said, "No, I don't think he died on purpose, but I do think he could have, might have prevented it. I know his lifestyle wasn't conductive to living a long life, but once AIDS became known, he certainly could have changed his living habits!"

Michael looks at me for the longest time. Finally, he takes my face in his hands and tells me he thinks I'm not being fair.

"But—" I stutter. He places one finger over my lips, ending my protest.

"What if," he says, "what if Freddie had such unwavering trust in you that he felt so safe in your love and support he knew he could live his life at the end the same way he lived the rest of it?

"What if he wanted to spare you the knowledge of what was coming because he felt a responsibility to protect you? What if he knew that because you had loved and supported him in the past, you would have the strength to face the future without him?

"What if his actions were a direct result of his faith in you? All of you! In every single Queen fan? In you personally, for that matter, for all you know Jacky could have told him about you, but consider this, woman, what's going on inside of you is eating you alive."

***

It nearly killed me, but I had to admit Michael was right. I did survive. I am surviving. I still miss you, and sometimes late at night, when I can't sleep, I cry over it. The empty spot.

I realize, now, that I am a very lucky person. The girl who introduced me to Queen is still a good friend. I've met people I never would have met, if it hadn't been for the fact that we loved the band. I have the memories, and my CDs and records, some videos and a bunch of magazine articles that are a permanent history of your life.

I have your example. Of the way you treated those close to you. The way you had the courage to follow your dreams and the way you never took no for an answer.

I learned to not take things for granted. Never again will I hesitate to tell someone that they matter to me. I try to treat people better, and I try to look out for the other guy.

I learned about courage and about not giving up on a dream. I learned to not let people tell me there was something wrong with me just because I am different, and I learned to laugh. And trust.

But most importantly, I learned that if I can raise my children to live their lives with half the self-esteem, courage, dignity and humor in which you lived yours, I will be a successful parent.

Good-bye my friend. Peace be with you.

Love always,
M.

(This is dedicated to Queen fans the world over.)

RAMBLINGS OF
A RELUCTANT LIBRARIAN

by Steve Kenworthy

One day, not too long ago I had a short conversation with my six-year-old son. It started with a question from him that caught me quite off-guard. "Dad," he asked, "why didn't you grow up to BE anything?"

My first response was to crawl into bed and wallow in self-pity for the rest of my natural existence. But, being a glutton for torture, I ventured, "What do you mean?"

"Well, like a fireman or a policeman," he replied.

I could have stopped right there, but my sense of self-pride made me blurt out, "But I am a librarian."

I fully expected a polite but disappointed "Oh." from my son. Instead, his eyes brightened, a broad smile spread across his innocent face and he said, "Really? Wow!" and ran off satisfied that his Dad was not a loser but was SOMETHING.

It took me a long time to admit to myself that I was a librarian. But this book gives me the perfect opportunity to climb up on my soap box and defend my profession and its necessity in society.

As a young boy, I knew that librarians existed but I had this strange impression that they were just made, that nobody really grew up to be a librarian.

My mother used to take me to the library. My first visits were to the Sonoma County Library in Santa Rosa, California. The library was housed among the county administrative buildings. All the county agencies like zoning, planning, records, etc., were housed in the complex and the library occupied one small wing. I liked to go to the library. I always got books with lots and lots of pictures.

When I was seven years old the county constructed a new library downtown. This library was a lot nicer but farther away, so the frequency of our visits decreased. The public schools I attended maintained libraries. I can't remember what the insides of the libraries at my junior high and high schools looked like. I was vaguely aware of the libraries. I'm pretty sure I even went in them once or twice (usually as a shortcut through one of the buildings). Eventually the county built a branch library 150 yards from my home, but by that time I had lost interest in libraries. Libraries had become unnecessary, uncool, and unappealing. I didn't even like the books with lots and lots of pictures anymore.

Not once growing up, regardless of my ever-changing opinion of libraries, had I considered becoming a librarian. The thought never crossed my mind. Like all little boys, I dreamed about what I wanted to be when I grew up, but becoming a librarian was beyond my imagination. If anyone had suggested during my teen years that I would become a librarian, I would have laughed myself into apoplexy.

At one time or another, I considered, and worked toward becoming: A pest control operator (succeeding my father, "Killer Ken"); an actor ("To be, or not to be. That is the question."); a lawyer (please don't hold that against me); a television director (my college major); and a video store owner (I love movies). You will notice that there is no librarian in that list.

I was thirty years old before I realized that a person could grow up to be a librarian. By that time I had already worked part-time in a library for three years. (Some of us are a little slow on the uptake.) I was offered a permanent, full-time position in the library where I had worked. I had an epiphany. People DECIDE to become librarians! I decided to become a librarian. But I admit that this decision was more because I needed a job to feed my family than because I wanted to be a librarian.

Maybe it is simply to justify my existence, but during the ensuing years I have come to appreciate the profession of librarianship. I've found that a librarian is more than a "stamper of books."

So, what is a librarian? A librarian is a guide to information. Mounds and mounds of information are produced every day by authors, journalists, politicians, media producers and the like. A vast jungle of entangled threads of obscure information daunts even the courageous questioner. A librarian is trained to direct you to sources that answer your questions. Librarians don't know everything—they just know where to find the answers.

A librarian is a guardian of free speech. In the jungle of information there are many conflicting points of view. A librarian's job is to make all points of view on a topic available so that people have the information necessary to form educated opinions. Librarians don't judge—they provide access to the information so that you can make an honest judgment.

A librarian is a teacher. Information is useless unless a person can access it and use it. Librarians must teach access and use of information. Librarians teach men, women and children. They teach professionals, laborers, and handicapped. Librarians don't give you information—they teach you where it is and how to use it.

A librarian is a public servant. A librarian strives to meet the needs of the patrons. Many times those needs are information, but they also may be needs for a listening ear, a warm reception, a place to feel important. The librarian serves without respect to race, religion, gender, age, intelligence, sexual orientation, or on which side of the head a person parts the hair. Librarians don't see men, women, Catholics, Jews, or Protestants—they just see people.

A librarian is a person. A librarian is not made, not hatched, not born of an alien species. A librarian is a flesh and blood human being who cares about the intellectual and cultural improvement of the community and the world. Librarians don't need to change the world—they just want to make it a little better place to live.

I am a librarian. I'm glad my six-year-old thinks that's special. But whether or not he does, I know that I have grown up to be SOMEBODY.

***

A few people don't agree with me. I'll point this out by referring to my favorite demographic—lawyers. What's the difference between a lawyer and a vulture? The lawyer takes off his wing tips at night. There are really only two lawyer jokes—the rest are all true. I have a collection of thousands of lawyer jokes (or true stories if you believe the latter). I love them. I've worked for and around lawyers for years and collecting the jokes was one way of keeping my sanity. Most of the jokes are based on a well-developed stereotype for lawyers. There is a similarly well developed stereotype for librarians. It's just that no one makes jokes about it. What's the difference between a librarian and a bump on a log? Nothing. See? Not funny.

Hollywood has just announced a new movie. This movie is about two mild-mannered librarians, a man and a woman who fall hopelessly in love. Who do you think will play the leads? Would you believe Harrison Ford and Meg Ryan? How about Tom Hanks and Julia Roberts? Let's be more realistic: George Boring and Linda Plain. Face it. People don't think glamour in the same sentence with librarian.

As far as I know Hollywood isn't really planning such a picture. Librarians don't create box office receipts. Librarians have had their share of movie roles, though. Unfortunately, most mass media depictions of librarians perpetuate the stereotype of a meek, fastidious, prudish person more interested in books than in having a life.

I guess we've established that librarians are not funny and they're not glamorous. At least if you believe the perpetuated mass media image of librarians.

Recently I came across an article written by Stephen Walker and V. Lonnie Lawson entitled, "The Librarian Stereotype and the Movies." Some of what immediately follows was inspired by (i.e., taken from) that article.

Years ago on the television game show "Family Feud" 100 people were surveyed as to what they believed were the typical librarian characteristics. The top five answers, in order, were: 1) Quiet; 2) Mean or Stern; 3) Single/Unmarried; 4) Stuffy; 5) Wears glasses.

You now have the perfect image of a librarian. That image came from the popular media. Think of Marian the librarian in "The Music Man." She is introduced as quiet, stern, single, stuffy and wearing glasses. But thanks to the attentions of a con man she is transformed into a vivacious, beautiful, out-going real person who can see just fine. She probably had to give up her job at the library.

The opening scene of "Ghostbusters" took place in the New York Public Library. Both the human and ghostly librarians were displayed as stereotypes. Bill Murray's questioning of the human librarian demonstrated just what he thought of librarians.

Even the great director Alfred Hitchcock was not beyond using a stereotypical librarian. In his 1943 classic, "Shadow of a Doubt," he has a scene in a library where the librarian is a late middle-aged female with hair pulled back in a tight bun, who talks to the lead character (a young adult) as if she were a kindergartner.

But the best stereotypical film portrayal of a librarian comes from Frank Capra's "It's a Wonderful Life." After George Bailey is granted his wish to have never been born, he goes off in search of his family and friends. It comes down to finding his wife. He begs Clarence, the angel, to let him see his wife. "You're not going to like it," says Clarence. "She's a librarian!" And then we see that poor Mary, after never meeting George, became an old maid, tied her hair in bun, took to wearing glasses and lost all of her vivaciousness. . . just so she could work in a library.

I consider myself typical. I am a librarian. So, I will put myself to the test:

1) QUIET: This is a very subjective criterion. How quiet is quiet. I hate to whisper. I love to laugh. I will interrupt the most solemn occasions to crack a joke. The only time I'm quiet is in church—but even then my snoring may disqualify me.

2) MEAN or STERN: I am not mean, stern or strict. Just ask anyone. Except my kids.

3) SINGLE/UNMARRIED: Sorry. I married Karen in 1982. We're still happily married and the parents of six children.

4) STUFFY: We're talking about a guy whose windpipe goes into convulsions whenever he comes within ten feet of a necktie. If you consider blue jeans and cowboy boots stuffy. . .well, what can I say?

5) WEARS GLASSES: Sorry again. No glasses. No contact lenses. Just my pretty blues.

There is one more overwhelming stereotype of the librarian: librarians are female. This has some statistical support. 83% of professional librarians are female. The percentage is even higher for library paraprofessionals. In fact, librarianship is the most female dominant occupation. More so than nursing or teaching. But here, too, I fall short. Maybe I'll have to give up my job as a librarian. I can't seem to fit any of the stereotypes.

If you're interested in catching a few librarians on film, here is an incomplete filmography:

Foul Play	Colin Higgins	1978
Ghostbusters	Ivan Reitman	1984
Indiana Jones & the Last Crusade	Steven Spielberg	1989

It's a Wonderful Life	Frank Capra	1946
The Music Man	Morton DeCosta	1962
Off Beat	Michael Dinner	1986
Shadow of a Doubt	Alfred Hitchcock	1943
Something Wicked This Way Comes	Jack Clayton	1983

Just remember, few, if any, librarians are stereotypical. I wear jeans, I have been known to smile, and my hair isn't pulled back in bun.

***

Have you ever tried to force a child to eat her vegetables. It can't be done. A child's willpower and imagination can outlast a parent's resolve and determination. I know that the "hide-the-vegetables" game gave my own imagination a first-class workout. My own children are even more inventive. I have one child who likes to sit at a particular end of the table. . . just a quick toss away from the garbage can. Another child thought that if he kept throwing scraps under the table maybe we'd take the hint and buy a dog. I had one child who kept a chewed up carrot in his mouth for three days. He played, ate and slept with carrot mulch. He was allowed finally to spit it out. No, you can't force a child to eat his vegetables.

As a child I heard, and as a parent I use, all of the persuasive arguments for eating vegetables. "Think of all the poor starving people in China." "They're good for you." "Where would Popeye be if he didn't eat his spinach." But, until a kid decides that his body wants and needs vegetables, there will be an ugly struggle at the dinner table. And nobody wins.

Few children want to eat their vegetables. Lets face it, many adults don't want to eat their vegetables. Vegetables just don't taste as good as a Hershey bar. Sadly, many people view reading good books as a lot like eating their vegetables. They would much rather spend their time on the literary chocolate bars.

I am guilty, as charged. I prefer reading a popular novel that zips right along than dig into a novel that makes me think, re-read passages, and evaluate my beliefs. My approach to non-fiction is much the same. This pattern even manifests itself when I read newspapers. I will pick up "USA Today" before I'll touch the "Wall Street

Journal."

In junior high and high school I had a required reading list that was fairly typical back then. You probably had to read a few of them yourself. *1984* and *Animal Farm* by George Orwell; *A Separate Peace* by John Knowles; J.D. Salinger's *Catcher in the Rye;* several works by Mark Twain; John Steinbeck's *Of Mice and Men;* and others by Kafka, Huxley, Shakespeare, Dumas. I've missed a few but these are the works that most would classify as "classics."

The difference between me and my classmates is that I never read any of those books before graduating from high school. No, not one. I never read a novel for a class assignment. You're probably thinking that I had the grades to prove it. On the contrary. I got straight A's in English and literature classes. I wrote book reports and comparative essays. I participated in classroom discussions. I enrolled in advanced classes and even passed the Advanced Placement exam in English for college credit. I didn't learn of Cliff Notes until I was in college. I was just adept at hiding my vegetables.

Being told to read a book referred to as a classic or as an important work was tantamount to being told to eat my vegetables. Deep down I knew they were good for me, but I couldn't bring myself to partake when there were so many "goodies" lying around, waiting for me to devour them.

Then I got into a college philosophy class where the teacher sparked my interest in a couple of the above mentioned titles. I thought maybe I'd try one. I read George Orwell's *1984.* It wasn't too bad. In fact, I enjoyed it. Not only did it have a compelling story, but I found that thinking while reading was not nearly as painful as I had anticipated. Then I read Kafka's *The Castle.* That was a real struggle. But when I was finished I felt I had accomplished something. I felt stronger. I had eaten my literary spinach. I decided to explore the other works of literature that I had previously avoided.

In adulthood I have completed my high school reading list. Not because I had to, but because I wanted to. I'm the only person I know that has read Kafka as recreational reading and not as a classroom assignment. I've read the complete works of William Shakespeare, I've read O. Henry, Faulkner, and a lot more.

Despite these claims and my occupation, I do not consider myself an avid reader. My wife reads much more than I do. My mother and sister read several novels a week. I have yet to ask my brother about a book he hasn't read—fiction or non-fiction. Most people I associate with read more than I do. But, I enjoy reading. I will and do read just about anything.

The funny part is, I still prefer the literary chocolate bars. I read mysteries, romances, adventures, horror, and non-fiction (my favorite subjects are biographies, politics and film history). But, at least now I'm no longer hesitant to eat my literary spinach. I appreciate the variety and I'm getting better at deciphering what's good taste and what tastes good.

There is nothing wrong with light-weight reading. You should read what you enjoy. I am an advocate of reading anything that sparks even the slightest interest. There is also nothing wrong with heavier reading. You just need to learn to enjoy that, too. The next time you come to visit the library, seek out something new and challenging. Read a classic. The librarian can help you and you'll feel healthier for having eaten your vegetables.

***

I have a friend whom I haven't seen in almost 15 years. He came to mind as I write this because he is the perfect example of the next library topic I want to discuss. "Gus" was (and I guess he still is) a nice guy. He wasn't the brightest guy in the world, but he could actively participate in conversation (particularly if the subject was sports or cars). I knew Gus from the time we were both toddlers. We went to the same church, played on the same sports teams, and graduated from high school together. After high school we went our separate directions and have since lost touch. I'd write Gus a letter but I don't think he would or could write back. Gus is illiterate.

One of the major concerns of librarians throughout the country is the literacy of the populace. Mr. Webster gives the definition of literacy as "the ability to read and write." In the past decade illiterates graduating from high school and even college have been the subjects of numerous human interest news stories. Some surveys have placed the number of illiterate people in the United States at around 5 million people. I think the number is much higher.

Of course, I would define literacy as the ability to communicate with a written language. My definition takes the ability to read and write one step further and requires a person to be able to process thoughts in writing. Someone who reads an article or a book should gain some insight into the thoughts of the author. There should be comprehension, not only on a surface level, but also on a conceptual level. If this does not occur, then the writer or the reader, or both are illiterate.

My friend Gus can read and write, but he can't communicate with the written word. He can read almost anything, slowly, but he can't understand what he reads. He can fill out a simple application, but he can't write a coherent sentence. Gus is just literate enough to make it through life, but he is missing out on the many wonderful experiences afforded by true literacy.

I have never known Gus to read a book, newspaper, or magazine for pleasure. Television fills most of his information and entertainment needs. Movies, friends, or colleagues fill in the rest. Gus doesn't have an inkling of what goes on in the world outside of his own, limited sphere. He doesn't dream of great things. He doesn't wonder about the mysteries of life. It is difficult for him to participate in the democratic process. I imagine, at the heart of the matter, Gus feels very isolated and lonely.

Gus doesn't write either. The weight of a pen or pencil in his hand is as foreign as a rainstorm in the Sahara. What legacy will he leave his posterity? No journal, no letters, no prose, no poetry.

Gus' situation is sad. But I have another acquaintance whose situation may be even worse. "Mac" has a college education. He is literate in the strict sense of the word. But the day he graduated from college was the day he decided he'd had enough learning and vowed never to pick up a book again. Mac refuses to read. He thinks life is too short for sitting around reading. There are "none so blind as those that will not see." Mac is not illiterate by circumstance, he is illiterate by choice.

Illiteracy is damning. It stops our progress. It hinders our ability to reach our potential. Those 5 million illiterate Americans and the millions more like Gus & Mac go through life in a myopic stupor, blind to so much of the beauty around them. My heart cries for them. But that is not enough. I want to help open their eyes to the world of literacy. What can I do?

I decided that the first thing I must do is encourage literacy in myself. This means developing the discipline to read and write every day. Finding things I enjoy will help establish the habit. Finding new materials will eliminate any risk of tediousness.

After I am converted I must encourage literacy in my family. It is easy to convince my wife and children to read because they enjoy it. The children that are too small to read are read to. I've never had one refuse to sit down and listen to a story.

It is more difficult to prod my family into writing. I try to encourage journals and letter writing as the most interesting and easiest forms of writing. I try to be enthusiastic when family members show some initiative in creative writing. Most important of all is the discussion of what we read and write. Talking about it raises our interest level and demonstrates the support structure we have created for each other.

When my family is happily skipping down the road to literacy I need to focus my attention outward to my circle of friends and acquaintances. And from there into the community at large. I'll already have lots of practice from training myself and my family. It is amazing what influence we have sharing our success with others. Recommending a novel or mentioning a magazine article could be the impetus to get Mac to start reading again. Maybe a letter of encouragement will help Gus realize he can expand his horizons. Volunteering with county and state social agencies may lead us to help those who have not had the educational advantages. Whatever we choose to do, we must do something.

Literacy is more than reading and writing. It is a vision of the world that is bright and hopeful. Share your abilities to help someone see the light. Maybe I'll sit down and write Gus a letter.

***

I'll let you in on a little secret. The library has a severe shortage of librarians. In fact, only one librarian works at the Whitman County Rural Library. Me. Already I can hear the cries of protest clambering from the depths of your bowels. "What about Pat? What about Kristie? What about Cindy, Peggy & Shirley? What about all the branch managers? What about Laura, Neva Jean, Marie, Jerri,

Marva & Gene?" Well, it is my job to inform you that, according to the American Library Association (ALA), they are not librarians. The best they can hope for is a classification as "paraprofessionals." Most would be classified as clerks or pages. If they call themselves librarians a hit squad of old maid librarians, with their hair tied properly in buns, will descend upon them and clobber them with unabridged dictionaries.

In an attempt to raise the status of librarians the ALA has set up criteria that a person must meet to call themselves a librarian. By establishing these criteria the ALA has presumed to create a "profession." According to the ALA a librarian should be viewed on the same level as doctors and lawyers. (Despite that opening, I'll leave the lawyer jokes alone for now.) The one established criterion that I meet and that no one else on our staff meets, is having earned a masters level "professional" degree. . . known commonly as an MLS (Master of Library Science). The ALA creates the standards for the MLS and accredits universities that offer library degrees. I got this job partly because I have an ALA accredited MLS.

Actually, my degree is an MLIS, a Master of Library and Information Sciences. I can use these letters after my name to command respect and awe from all I meet. Imagine a few business cards you might see:

> Dr. Sam Paine, MD
> Dewey Cheatham, JD
> Rev. Wade Jordan, Mdiv

Now try this:

> Steve Kenworthy, MLIS

Fits right in, don't you think? I don't either. I believe that this campaign of the ALA exists simply to justify their vanity on the backs of all the non-degreed professionals who were too busy doing library work to take a year or two off to go to school to learn what they already know.

To assert that the MLS degree requires a similar effort, knowledge and skill as a Juris Doctorate, Master of Business Administration or medical degree is arrogant, pretentious, and erroneous. Having attended both library school and law school, I will tell you plainly that there is no comparison. Any person with a basic, high school education could do the work required for an MLS degree. Although my peers consider this heresy and blasphemy, the truth is that the Master of Library Science program taught at the library schools of prestigious universities around the country is not a post-graduate curriculum but simply a glorified technical program.

Now that I've alienated 30,000 librarians, I'll tell you how I define professionalism in libraries. A professional librarian has a service-oriented attitude combined with proficiency in knowing and using a collection. By this definition many MLS degree holders fail to qualify as professionals. One "librarian" of my acquaintance refuses to work at the reference or circulation desks at his library because he is a "professional" and the duties performed by lowly desk personnel are beneath his exalted status.

A librarian must care about information and ideas. A librarian must care even more about people. But most of all, a librarian must care about putting information, ideas and people together. This caring requires that a librarian know what sources are in the library collection and how to use them. It requires a librarian to be familiar with fiction, children's works and the authors that produce them. It requires a librarian to be familiar and proficient with retrieval systems so that time is not wasted in filling the information needs of a patron. It requires a librarian to be a counselor and interviewer to adequately determine what a patron wants and needs. It requires a librarian to smile, be friendly and courteous, and treat all people equally.

Education is important for librarians. I'd recommend a college degree in the sciences or humanities with a broad liberal arts base. The bachelor degree provides a better foundation for librarianship than the MLS ever has or will. Of course, it is also necessary for librarians to learn the tricks of the trade. But I learned more about libraries in 6 weeks on the job than I did in my 38 credit hours of graduate library school studies.

A professional librarian has an interest in librarianship as a whole. They take the time to read the literature of the profession. They hobnob with fellow librarians to see what is happening in other libraries. They share their own ideas to improve service at home and in all libraries. You could say that they are helpful, kind, courteous, thrifty, and honest but the Boy Scouts have already secured that string of adjectives.

It is easy to earn an MLS degree. Thousands do it every year. It is ludicrous to base professional status on that degree. It is not easy to be a professional librarian. It takes desire and hard work. It takes a special person with a respect for literacy and a love for people. It does not take a diploma.

The Whitman County Library employs many librarians. Professional librarians. A college degree doesn't create a professional. An MLS degree isn't worth the paper it's printed on. A smile, a lot of enthusiastically applied elbow grease, and a significant pay increase will do more to raise the status of librarians than adding some letters to the end of a person's name. As for its definition of a librarian, the American Library Association can go . . . fly a kite.

***

I still wonder at the strange turn of events that have brought me into this profession. I'm sure, if I had it all to do over again, I'd still try to pursue other career choices. Deep down I just can't conceive of anyone choosing to be a librarian. On the other hand, I have gained a profound sense of satisfaction and contentment since accepting my fate. I am happier as a librarian than I have ever been in my life. Not wealthier, just happier.